Praise for
Charlene Donaghy's
Bones of Home and Other Plays

With plays that are intoxicating and mysterious, Donaghy has a gift for finding the truth that lurks below our eccentricities.

> Doug Wright, Pulitzer Prize and
> Tony Award winning playwright

Donaghy is a fearless explorer of human nature. Whether her characters live in New Orleans on a set of concrete steps, on a dilapidated porch in Provincetown, or even on another plane of existence, they never cease to ask the big questions, and the answers always come from the heart.

> Kate Snodgrass, Artistic Director,
> Boston Playwrights Theatre

Charlene writes stories that give voice beyond the boundaries of race, sex, or privilege, painting pictures of human conditions, taking her audiences on journeys through the gift and magic of her words.

> Jackie Davis, Artistic Director,
> New Urban Theatre Laboratory, Actor

With her unique voice, Charlene captures the raw, human emotions of love, loss, and longing. We root for her complex beautiful characters, right until the very last moment when we are left breathless with our own emotions rising to the surface.

> Ronan Noone, author, *The Atheist,*
> *The Second Girl, Scenes from an Adultery*

Charlene is not afraid to take her readers and audience to the dark places—whether that's during a contentious time in history, a city's complex past or a character's uncontrollable desire. For it is through her exploration of the dark, that Charlene ultimately shows us the light in all of humanity.

Jami Brandli, author, *Technicolor Life*,
BLISS (or Emily Post is Dead!) and *¡SOLDADERA!*

The Quadroon and the Dove gives audiences "...a close up look at not only the lengths people will go to attain their heart's desire, but the obsessions that drive them there."

Melissa Wrap, *The Memphis Daily Helmsman*

Gift of an Orange: In a good play nothing goes the way you think it will, and all you can hope for is to be spellbound for however long the action continues and to walk out unsure of what you are feeling but knowing you are feeling something. This play delivers on all counts.

Sue Harrison, *The Cape Codder* and *Provincetown Banner*

BONES of HOME

& OTHER PLAYS

BONES of
HOME
& OTHER PLAYS

CHARLENE A. DONAGHY

HANSEN PUBLISHING GROUP, LLC

ISBN (trade paper) 978-1-60182-260-4
ISBN (ebook) 978-1-60182-261-1

Cover photograph © 2015 David Halliday
http://www.davidhallidayphotography.com

Illustrations © 2015 Cynthia Secof Hersch

Cover and book interior design by Jon Hansen

Hansen Publishing Group, LLC
302 Ryders Lane
East Brunswick, NJ 08816

http://hansenpublishing.com

To Mom & Dad for encouraging me to dream.

To Gary and my girls for always supporting my dreams.

To Proscenium, 9th Floor, and my fellow theatre artists for sharing the art of dreams.

To New Orleans, her stories, and her people for inspiring my dreams.

CONTENTS

Foreword... xi
Preface xiii
Acknowledgements... xv
Production Premieres xvi
Style Notes.. xviii

TEN MINUTE PLAYS

White Bra with a Pink Bow 5
Broken Wings on St. Maurice 13
Sliding 20
Freak Out 28
Bones of Home... 37
Who You Got to Believe... 46
Proverbs 55

ONE ACTS PLAYS

Gift of an Orange.. 65
Another August.. 92
Sword Play.. 108
Jingle of a Moment 121

FULL LENGTH

The Quadroon and the Dove 133

LAGNIAPPE

I Like 221
Tomato 224
Joanie & Freddie on Valentine's Day.................................... 228

About the Author... 238

FOREWORD

Along the way, every playwright searches the landscape for road signs to suggest, "Yes, I'm making progress. I'm going in the right direction." For some writers, those signs happen few and far between (leaving the writer to wonder if the effort is worth the heartache); for others, those signs come in measured increments that gives the writer the hope and energy to push forward, to work harder, to struggle for one more month or year. And still for others, the signs (of success, if you can see it that way) come one right after the other.

Having a collection of plays published is a huge sign that the writer is on the right path, that all the years of writing, waiting, wondering and hoping that someone (a producer, a theatre, a publisher) recognizes the value in what you've written and wants to share that with a larger community, have finally paid off. Charlene Donaghy has met a mark in *Bones of Home*, a mark that not only nods to her muse and constant source of inspiration, New Orleans, but her skill at writing intricately detailed characters that suffer through the worst and celebrate the best of being human (read *The Quadroon and The Dove* and see if you don't agree).

What I love about this collection of plays is the broad range of writing styles, from the Williams inspired *Gift of an Orange*, to a coming-of-age innocence in *White Bra With a Pink Bow*, to the searing realism of *The Quadroon and the Dove*. It takes a master craftsperson to find not only her voice as a writer (what does she want to say), but the individual voices of those she creates (how she wants to say it). Charlene Donaghy is offering you expertise in both.

I hope you enjoy this collection as much as I did. And then I hope you'll do all writers a solid, and recommend it to someone else to read. We need that kind of support as writers; it's what keep us strong, moves us forward and advances the writer as a primary artist of the theatre.

Gary Garrison
New York City, 2015

PREFACE

I am drawn to New Orleans splendor and her decay. And as any New Orleanian or adopted child of the city knows, there are many times when splendor and decay intertwine. *Bones of Home and Other Plays* weaves these together with history and present day, sometimes spiraling out from New Orleans center like the delicate threads of a web.

My contemporary plays spring forth from the questions of our times. How does the downward economy change family dynamics? How can uncontrollable crime bring people together? How does our penchant for youth at all costs influence friendships? How can a lonely soul find strength within? These are questions we ask when faced with conditions that can be both commonplace and rare.

My historic plays, complicated by Louisiana lore, yet resonant with the present, offer a look at what remains the same and what changes through the years. We all want love and security and, sometimes, we go to dark places to hold onto them. Whether 1841, 1972, or anytime in between, my historic plays resonate with struggles we continue to confront today, amid themes of race, gender, and power.

I adopted New Orleans (or did she adopt me?) one unforgettable autumn when, at a young age, I was undergoing chemotherapy for breast cancer. In my recovery, I joined a book club and the first authors we read drew inspiration from New Orleans: I was hooked. I scoured bookshelves and began a library of Crescent City authors: from Lafcadio Hearn to Julie Smith, from Zora Neale Hurston to Andrei Codrescu, from Lillian Hellman to Chris Rose.

And, of course, from Faulkner to Williams and beyond. From these authors I gained strength.

From New Orleans many angles—her people, culture, architecture, history, food, music—I have gained a home where, in some ways, I am more myself than in any other place. And, in other ways, I am from elsewhere. It is a dichotomy that feeds me as an artist. It also propels me to respect my like-characters as well as those whose truths I cannot know from within. I embrace their lives, complicated by choices between disparate worlds, with care and a hunger to explore. Because I feel the light enhances the dark, those choices are about good and evil, hope and loss, faith and doubt...and they usually involve a search for the meaning of home.

I am fortunate to have found home in many places. In Connecticut, where I was born and raised, my husband, dogs, and family are my heart of home. In Tennessee, the Smoky Mountains give me peace of home. I find an ethereal light of home in Provincetown, Massachusetts. With my fellow theatre artists in Boston and New York I have an alliance of home. And New Orleans, with her *Bones of Home*, is the place where I dream the stories I craft. This collection of plays intertwines to form the threads of my art, coming from all of my homes and their inspirations.

Charlene A. Donaghy
Bones of Home and Other Plays

ACKNOWLEDGEMENTS

A good gumbo takes time and patience, a multitude of ingredients, and sometimes the best ones come together with many hands in the pot. The gumbo of *Bones of Home and Other Plays* was created in just such a way with hands and hearts of support, tough love, kindness, laughter, and much more. My core groups of writers, Boston's Proscenium Playwrights and New York City's 9th Floor, are the knowledgeable sounding boards for my craft. Over the years I've been fortunate to have writing and theatre mentors who have pushed me forward: Jami Brandli, Rickey Gard Diamond, Tony Eprile, Jef Hall-Flavin, Gary Garrison, Laban Carrick Hill, David Kaplan, Kate Snodgrass, Jessica Treat, Gavin Witt—to name but a few. I've been blessed with a multitude of directors who understand my voice and my stories, including two who have brought my characters to life numerous times: Jackie Davis and Paul Revaz. I've grown my knowledge of production in my work with the Provincetown Tennessee Williams Theater Festival and The Warner International Playwrights Festival. There have been women in my life who have taught me courage and the love of friendship: Mary Conroy, Vicki Daly, Robbi D'Allessandro, Sharon Dante, Kim Samele, Julie Weinberg, the Lesley Golden Girls, and the University of Nebraska and Vermont College ladies, to name but a few. Finally, this book is made possible because of my amazing family that applauds the challenges and successes: dad Fred, mom Joan, sisters Cynthia, Connie, Clarissa, cousin Wendy, especially my most supportive, loving husband Gary, and my furry kids who, no matter how many times I come and go for my art, always greet me with the exuberance that can only be found in happily wagging tails, soft bellies for gentle rubs, and noses that can always detect the bouquet of a good gumbo.

PRODUCTION PREMIERES

WHITE BRA WITH A PINK BOW: Warner International Playwrights Festival, Connecticut. Directed by Jackie Davis. Starring Marie Roy-Daniels as Becca, Elizabeth Keise as Tammy, and Laura Honeywood as Kim. First published in *25*10-Minute Plays for Teens*, edited by Lawrence Harbison, Applause Theatre & Cinema Books.

BROKEN WINGS ON ST. MAURICE: New Urban Theatre Laboratory's 5 & Dime, Boston, MA. Directed by Jackie Davis. Starring Jojo Kindeur as Maggie and Richard Caines as Trey.

SLIDING: Commissioned by Three Tattoos, New York City. BoCoCa Arts Festival. Directed by Sarah V. Michelson. Starring Mateo Moreno as Eric and Jessica Vera as Tanya.

FREAK OUT: Towne Street Theatre, Los Angeles, CA. Directed by Raf Mauro. Starring Nancy Cheryl Davis-Bellamy as Becca, Nancy Renee as Tammy, and Diane Sellers as Kim.

BONES OF HOME: West Coast Players Theatre, Clearwater, FL. Directed by Don Hebert. Starring Tory Goss as Dillon and Mabel LaCola as Miriam.

WHO YOU GOT TO BELIEVE: Kansas City Women's Playwriting Festival. Directed by Richard Alan Nichols. Starring Glendora Davis as Kathleen and Sanford Kelly as Ray. First published in *Best American Short Plays 2009-2010*, edited by Barbara Parisi, Applause Theatre & Cinema Books

PROVERBS: New York City's Poor Mouth Theatre Company's Puttin' on Your Shorts. Directed by Paul Revaz. Starring Jane

Coughlin as Eulalie, Jamal Ford-Bey as Claude, Keith Paul as The Horseman.

GIFT OF AN ORANGE: New Urban Theatre Laboratory, Boston, MA and The Provincetown Tennessee Williams Theater Festival. Directed by Jackie Davis. Starring Dayenne C. Byron Walters as Oshun, Richard Caines as Taurean, and James Bocock as Jake. First published in *Best American Short Plays 2011-2012*, edited by William W. Demastas, Applause Theatre & Cinema Books.

ANOTHER AUGUST: Know Theatre, Binghamton, NY. Directed by Tim Gleason. Starring Jason Walsh as Jimmy, Qiana Watson as Ruby, and Foster Daniels, Jr. as Prentiss.

SWORD PLAY: Inspired by *Nürnberg Cathedral*, oil on panel, by Charles Hartley for Know Theatre's Artists and Playwrights Festival. Directed by Tim Gleason. Starring Katie Barlow as Maeve, Alfie Massey as Aaron/Amara and Rich Bocek as Father Dolan.

JINGLE OF A MOMENT: Chroma Productions' Collage, Boston, MA. Directed by Christopher Webb. Starring Jessica Webb as Hannah.

THE QUADROON AND THE DOVE: New York City Premiere, Madison Square Productions, 2016.

STYLE NOTES

Our intent is for Charlene Donaghy's plays to read more like liter-ature than an actor's script. There are notations used by the play-wrights in conveying the actions and interactions of the characters to the reader as well as to actors performing the play. For those readers who are unfamilar with these notations, we have placed the key here rather than repeat it with every play in this volume which would detract from the plays themselves.

//	Indicates characters speaking over each other
- -	Indicates one character cutting off the other's dialog
…	Indicates an incomplete or internal thought
Pause	Indicates a breath for consideration of the character's thoughts or action in that moment
Beat	Indicates a half-pause

BONES of
HOME

& OTHER PLAYS

Ten Minute Plays

WHITE BRA
WITH A PINK BOW

CAST OF CHARACTERS (ALL AGE 13)

BECCA: Shy. Wearing 1972-era gym shorts and top.

TAMMY: Boisterous. Wearing 1972-era gym shorts and top.

KIM: Athletic. Wearing bell bottoms, vintage NOLA sports team T-shirt.

TIME

Early autumn afternoon. New Orleans, LA. September, 1972.

SETTING

Junior High School girl's locker room. A locker room bench is center stage with a gym bag on the floor next to it. A large mirror is on stage or the fourth wall acts as a mirror.

PRODUCTION NOTES

All actors stay clothed during the play. The "pencil test" segments should be blocked over T-shirts.

Playwright gives permission for play personalization with city/town of production. Approved changes are: KIM'S vintage T-shirt to a local team, changing "Pontchartrain Park" to a local 1970s-era park hang-out, and changing "D.H. Holmes" to a local 1970s-era department store.

———————

In darkness, a locker room shower is heard.

Blue lights cascade onto the stage like shower water, turning white, then filling the stage with full light.

BECCA stands in front of mirror looking at herself, singing a line or two about "stars" from a song like "Walking in the Rain" by The Partridge Family.

Shower fades. BECCA moves hands to breasts, already developed far beyond her friends.

BECCA: If I have to grow up, please let me have little boobs like Laurie Partridge.

> *TAMMY enters, snaps a towel at BECCA.*

TAMMY: Ha! You'll never have Laurie Partridge boobs, birthday girl. You're already too big.

BECCA: Nut-uh!

TAMMY: Yeah-huh! You could entertain the troops in Vietnam with - -

BECCA: I wish I *could* go there.

TAMMY: Becca, I'm your best friend, right?

> *BECCA nods.*

TAMMY: It'd be far out if somebody could fix this but you can't live only for that day. Your dad wouldn't want you to. We're in eighth grade. Junior High top of the heap. And look at you. You need a bra! What a great birthday present!

BECCA: If I need a bra that means I can't stay ten years old. I promised I'd stay a little girl.

TAMMY: We haven't been ten years old - -

BECCA: In three years.

TAMMY: We're *teenagers* now. We're gonna go to eighth grade dances at Pontchartrain Park. With *boys*!

BECCA: I don't need any boys.

TAMMY: Yeah-huh. Can't stop time even if we wanna. Boobs are gonna grow…well, maybe not mine. (beat) If you can put a pencil under your boob and it stays, you need a bra.

BECCA: Who says?

TAMMY: All the ninth graders.

BECCA: Nut-uh.

TAMMY: Yeah-huh.

BECCA: Nut-uh.

TAMMY: Let's try.

BECCA: No.

TAMMY: Don't be a spaz. C'mon.

> *TAMMY rummages through gym bag, grabs a pencil, sticks it under her breast (see production note). It falls, clattering to floor (beat) as they stare at it.*

TAMMY: Bogus. Your turn.

BECCA: No!

TAMMY grabs at BECCA who turns away. TAMMY tickles BECCA who finally giggles and tickles her back.

BECCA: (laughing) Stop it.

TAMMY: (laughing) C'mon, Laurie Partridge!

BECCA: (laughing) Stop. Stop! Okay.

BECCA takes the pencil, places under breast (see production note). It stays. BEAT as they stare in mirror.

TAMMY: Neat! It's like it's glued there.

BECCA removes pencil, hands it to TAMMY.

TAMMY: I'm sorry I said that. About Vietnam. I mean.

KIM enters carrying her gym outfit and a tennis racket.

KIM: Our first gym class of eighth grade and they cancel it. At least we got to change. Did you see the new girl from California? She's looks like a surfer girl. Tan with the longest hair I've ever seen. I wonder if she plays tennis.

KIM puts gym outfit in the gym bag and swings the tennis racket.

KIM: Billie Jean King is playing Karry Melville Saturday. King is gonna rule. Be there or be square. Happy birthday, Becs.

TAMMY: Becca needs a bra.

KIM: What's that gotta to do with tennis?

TAMMY: Nothing. I'm just saying. We did the pencil test. (beat) Here's your pencil. (tosses pencil to KIM) Becca's lucky.

BECCA: Nut-uh.

TAMMY: Yeah-huh! Every boy in school is gonna wanna date you. Its like you grew watermelons this summer.

BECCA: I'm not getting a bra!

KIM: Who cares what boys want, anyway.

> *KIM tries to put the pencil under her breast (see production note) but it keeps falling back into her hand. She finally throws it into the gym bag.*

BECCA: My dad said I'll always be his girl. I don't need any boys.

TAMMY: I'd faint if someone like David Cassidy would just look at me. Did you see him on the cover of *Tiger Beat* last week? It was the "1972 Super Sweethearts Issue." He was wearing a leather jacket, sitting on a motorcycle. He's so bitchin'.

BECCA: I hate motorcycles.

TAMMY: Motorcycles are bitchin'.

KIM: Nobody's gonna wanna date you if you say bitchin'.

TAMMY: Okay. *Cool.* Is that what California girl would say?

> *TAMMY sticks tongue out at KIM. KIM reciprocates.*

BECCA: See. We don't have to grow up.

> *BECCA sticks tongue out at TAMMY and KIM.*

TAMMY: Yeah-huh. Let's go buy you a bra. We'll get something like in the back of J.C. Penney catalog //

BECCA: Tam.

TAMMY: Where the women have black bras or //

BECCA: Tam!

TAMMY: Ones with leopard spots or something with lace //

BECCA: Tammy!

TAMMY: You're gonna be so popular. We're gonna rule Junior High and by the time we get to be freshman - -

BECCA: *Tammy!*

TAMMY: What?

BECCA: I. Don't. Want. A. Bra!

KIM: We can't buy bras at J.C. Penney, anyways. What do you think, there's some magic box where you can, I don't know, find anything you wish for, point to it and it'll magically appear at your door?

BECCA: If I could do that I'd wish for something other than a stupid bra. Besides, we're thirteen. My mom would have to drive us to Penney's.

TAMMY: Bitch…I mean cool.

KIM: Your mom has leopard bras. She even has red ones. And purple.

TAMMY: (teasing) Spying?

KIM: Nut-uh. She washes 'em and hangs 'em in the bathroom. To dry.

BECCA: I don't want leopard or red or purple! If I have to have a stupid bra then I want one of those white ones with a pink bow in the middle. I'll bet Laurie Partridge wears a white one with a pink bow in the middle.

TAMMY: Boring!

BECCA: Nut-uh.

TAMMY: Yeah-huh.

BECCA: Nut-uh!

TAMMY: Yeah-huh! And I'm tellin' ya, leather-wearing boys want girls with leopard bras.

BECCA: I don't want leather-wearing boys.

TAMMY: I am *not* going to the eighth grade dances with you two. You're gonna have to get dates eventually. And you could have any boy in school.

BECCA: I'd want somebody like…

TAMMY: Like?

KIM: Why do we only talk about boys, lately?

TAMMY: Cuz we're *supposed* to talk about boys.

KIM: Not me.

TAMMY: Ever?

KIM sticks her tongue out at TAMMY.

TAMMY: Hope your face freezes that way.

BECCA: Like my dad.

TAMMY: You want her face to freeze like your dad?

BECCA: I wanna boy like my dad. Somebody who's brave and strong and will take me to Dairy Queen for Dilly Bars and listen to The Partridge Family with me. His last letter said they're his favorite band, too.

KIM: They're gonna find him. He's a pilot. He *is* brave and strong.

BECCA: The Air Force keeps telling us that. (beat) I don't think my mom wants him found. She never had leopard bras or rode motorcycles before he went to Vietnam.

KIM: Maybe she did and you just didn't know.

BECCA: Somewhere he's wishing on stars to come home. I know it. He has to be.

KIM: Sure he is.

BECCA: And I don't wanna date boys or grow up. I wanna be exactly like he remembers me.

TAMMY: He'd want you to grow up. Be a teenager. You can date somebody like Michael Jackson. It'll be...

TAMMY sings a line from a song like The Jackson Five's "A-B-C". KIM then joins in and they both sing a line. BECCA then joins in and all three sing a line. They giggle.

TAMMY: And we'll bicycle over to D.H. Holmes and get you a white bra with a pink bow. Okay?

BECCA: Do I have to?

TAMMY nods. BECCA nods slowly with her.

KIM: It'll be okay. I can maybe ask the new girl to go with us.

TAMMY: Nut-uh. (beat) But can I at least try on a leopard bra?

KIM: For your mosquito bites?

BECCA giggles.

Lights fade.

END OF PLAY

BROKEN WINGS ON ST. MAURICE

CAST OF CHARACTERS

MAGGIE: 22 years old. Thin, small, delicate. Dressed in muted colors: faded jeans, faded shirt.

TREY: 28 years old. Burly, tall, rugged. Dressed in police officer uniform.

TIME

Fat Tuesday. Present Day.

SETTING

New Orleans, LA. A dilapidated kitchen in a once flooded, long-vacant shotgun house. Two tattered vintage chairs with rusted metal legs and ripped flowered vinyl seats. Matching Formica-top ratty table. A bent pair of old, tattered fairy wings sits near the chairs.

———————

Dusky light illuminates the stage as MAGGIE haltingly wanders in dragging behind her a ripped-from-ground lilac plant. She hauls the plant onto the table, picks up fairy wings, puts them on. She twirls around then climbs up onto one of the chairs and stands, precariously. TREY enters, searching.

TREY: I've been searching the whole city for you. What are you doing way out here?

MAGGIE jumps to other chair.

TREY: What are you wearing?

MAGGIE: Butterfly wings.

TREY: Butterfly wings?

MAGGIE jumps to other chair.

MAGGIE: I'm flying around from chair to chair because I'm a butterfly playing on flowers.

TREY: You're just going back and forth.

MAGGIE: There used to be four chairs.

TREY: We should go. The party's starting soon.

MAGGIE: Did you find them?

TREY: You ask me that every day. Don't you think I'd tell you if I did?

MAGGIE: Six months. Today.

TREY: I was hoping you might not remember.

MAGGIE stares at TREY.

TREY: I'm sorry.

MAGGIE jumps to other chair.

TREY: Please be careful.

MAGGIE: I was careful. Didn't matter then. Does it matter now?

TREY: After banging my head against the brick walls of this city for a half a year trying to find the bastards, maybe not.

MAGGIE: So you *are* giving up. Just like that.

TREY: Six months isn't 'just like that'.

TREY smacks plant. MAGGIE kicks out at TREY and almost falls off chair.

MAGGIE: Don't touch that.

TREY: Please tell me you didn't rip this out of some Garden District mansion.

MAGGIE: What's my favorite flower?

TREY: What?

MAGGIE: My favorite flower. What is it?

TREY: What does that have to do with - -

MAGGIE: Lilacs. I'm planting this out front just like when I was a kid.

TREY: It'll never grow out here.

MAGGIE: This is the only place I feel safe. Where we grew up. Mom's Monday red beans and rice around our table. Sitting on our chairs. Dad cutting us bouquets of lilacs.

MAGGIE jumps to other chair.

TREY: The whole house smelled like lilacs. (beat) That was a long time ago. You gotta get your costume on.

MAGGIE: I'm a butterfly, just like when I was eight years old.

TREY: Those broken wings have been moldering here for years.

MAGGIE: I can fly away with *these* broken wings.

TREY: Mags. Please.

MAGGIE: Why do you even wanna go? We haven't done anything in years and *now* you wanna be part of the big spectacle.

TREY: Don't you think its important to go? Try to get some normalcy back?

MAGGIE: What the hell is that?

TREY reaches out, touches MAGGIE'S hand.

TREY: That's me and you, big brother, little sister, just like always. Dressing up for parties. Fighting over who gets the last lemon ice. Pushing each other on the swings at Lee Playground.

MAGGIE: Lee Playground is long gone.

TREY: But we're still here. Six months ago didn't change that.

MAGGIE: It changed everything.

TREY: You gotta work with me here Mags.

MAGGIE pushes TREY's hand away, jumps to other chair.

MAGGIE: Easy for you to say. It didn't happen to you.

TREY: Yes. It did. (pause) Tell me what to do to help you move forward.

MAGGIE: I don't want to move forward. I want to move back. Right back here on St. Maurice Avenue. Everything was safe when we lived here.

TREY: We haven't lived here on St. Maurice since we were kids.

MAGGIE: Before mom and dad died. Before the storm. Before the *crime*.

TREY: The house is falling down, flooded out, years of moldy stink - -

MAGGIE: It's my home! I'm safe here!

TREY: No. You're not. (beat) I'm sorry I couldn't find them.

MAGGIE: But you're my big brother. The cop. That's your job.

TREY: I know.

MAGGIE: It's New Orleans. You have to try harder.

TREY: Can't we start with just one night, this one Fat Tuesday night to go to the party and forget? We both need that.

MAGGIE: I don't know how.

MAGGIE jumps to other chair.

TREY: I don't know what else to do. I tried everything. We're understaffed. Too few resources. Working too many hours. Too many cases.

MAGGIE: Someone had to see or hear.

TREY: Witnesses? They either don't care or they're too scared to testify.

MAGGIE: I'd testify. I would.

TREY: I worked every resource I could think of.

MAGGIE: You *have* given up.

TREY: I wish all those countless hours looking at mug shots and rap sheets of every...rapist on file, combing over evidence...I wish it paid off. Found some kind of lead. I'm on the job twelve hours a day and for the last six months I didn't go home for hours after that.

MAGGIE: What?

PAUSE as TREY sighs, tired.

TREY: I worked the case on my own time.

MAGGIE: You never told me that.

TREY: I couldn't tell you. I wanted...*needed* to find them. I went through all the evidence over and over and over.

MAGGIE: Over and over and over.

TREY: I tried.

MAGGIE: And today you want to go to a Mardi Gras party.

TREY: It's Fat Tuesday! Something has to be normal!

MAGGIE: Because *I'm* not!

TREY: What?

MAGGIE: Not anymore!

TREY: That's not what I meant - -

MAGGIE: But that's the way it is! (beat) I didn't do anything.

TREY: I know.

MAGGIE: I was just running along the levee. Cornflower blue sky. Sun just starting to warm the morning. I spotted a whole cluster of buckeye butterflies. Stopped to look at them. I should have started running again as soon as they flew away. Should have. (pause) Then it was too late. Hands. Bodies. I couldn't run. Couldn't fly away. They broke my wings. I'll never be safe again. Never. Never //

MAGGIE jumps to other chair, then back and forth, over and over.

TREY: Mags. Stop //

MAGGIE: Never. Never. Never //

TREY: You're gonna get hurt //

MAGGIE: Never. Never //

TREY: You're scaring me //

MAGGIE: Never //

TREY: *Mags!*

> *TREY steps between the chairs, forcing MAGGIE to stop jumping.*

TREY: Forget the party. Just come home with me. I'll fix this old kitchen set. Find two more chairs so you can stay a butterfly for as long as you need. I'll even plant that lilac bush out here.

MAGGIE: You said it'd never grow out here.

TREY: I'll find a way.

MAGGIE: I need to feel safe.

> *TREY pushes the empty chair closer to hers so they are touching. He climbs up on top, stands.*

TREY: I'll fix everything.

MAGGIE: Promise?

> *TREY reaches over and adjusts MAGGIE'S wings.*

> *Lights fade.*

END OF PLAY

SLIDING

CAST OF CHARACTERS

ERIC: 55 years old African-American man dressed casually in jeans and a Saints sweatshirt. He is struggling with loneliness and self-worth after much loss.

TONYA: 28 years old African-American woman dressed casually and clean in jeans and sweater. She is an only child, driven, determined, but ultimately disconnected from the one person who she should count on.

CHARACTER NOTE

Although written as African-American, cast could be any any ethnicity.

TIME

A late-autumn evening. Present day.

SETTING

Lockport, LA. A beat-up old wooden child's swing-set with two swings and a slide.

SETTING NOTE

Set could be representational with two chairs and a ladder.

Lights come up in a warm glow of sunset. ERIC is dismantling swing-set, taking off a side-bar.

TONYA: (off-stage) Hello?

> *ERIC quickly hides tool, sits on one swing. TONYA enters from yard.*

ERIC: Look what the cat dragged in.

TONYA: You built me this, what? When I was three? Four? With just the right angle for sliding down fast, but not too fast. I haven't seen you out here—

ERIC: In at least six months, anyway.

> *TONYA crosses to sit on other swing.*

TONYA: (scratches her hands) Hasn't been easy for me, either. Dad.

ERIC: Dad? Not Eric. You must be wantin' somethin'?

TONYA: (scratches her hands) Why do you have to assume that?

ERIC: Drove all the way out here, must be important.

TONYA: Maybe I just came to see you. Ever think of that? (beat) Forget it.

ERIC: You got your mama's habit of scratchin' your hands when somethin' botherin' you. You're here. Might as well tell me.

PAUSE as they look at, and past, each other.

TONYA: Restaurant's been on a downhill slide for the last year.

ERIC: I told you restaurants are tough but, as usual, you didn't want to listen.

TONYA: You know what, never mind. I'll figure it out on my own.

ERIC: How's that been workin' for you?

TONYA: (sarcastically) Just great. (beat as she sighs) Laid off staff. I'm doing all the cooking. I tried re-financing but banks aren't giving loans. I was hoping that maybe you could... you might have some money I could borrow...against the house.

ERIC: (sighs) Wish I could help.

TONYA: You can. Dad.

ERIC: There's that word again.

ERIC rises, retrieves tool, works on dismantling the swing-set, taking off the swing he was sitting on.

TONYA: I know we haven't talked much in the last six months.

ERIC: Much?

TONYA: Will you just sit down and talk to me? What are you doing to my swing-set?

ERIC: Takin' it apart.

TONYA: Why?

ERIC: I, uh, I...sold the house.

TONYA: What? You can't sell it. It's home. You. Me. (beat) Mom.

ERIC: Got a place in the city. Just one room.

TONYA: From ten rooms to one? In New Orleans? You never wanted to leave Lockport.

ERIC: Maybe if you came around more often I could tell you things.

TONYA: What do you want me to do? Sell the restaurant and move out here? Be kinda tough to do that *now*, don't you think? But, hey, you want me closer, fine, maybe that will solve *everything*.

ERIC: Get off your sassy-horse. I'm still your father.

TONYA: And this is my home. Where I grew up. Where things were normal and we were a family before...before mom got sick.

ERIC: We *were* a family. *With* your mama. Don't know what you and me been for the last six months besides strangers.

TONYA: You can't sell the house.

ERIC: Cuz you need the money.

TONYA: No. Because this is where mom is. You can't sell my memories.

ERIC throws tool on ground.

ERIC: Your memories? You think this is easy, just one, two, three I'm outta here? You have no idea how lonely...I wake up every mornin' in our bed, holdin' your mama's pillow. I still put on a full pot of coffee even after all these months. I can't bring myself to put away her Mardi Gras costume cuz it was the last one she wore and that was a good week. One of the last good weeks. I feel her in this house, in these here walls.

TONYA: (scratches her hands) Then why? You need...*we* need a home. I need to know I can find mom here. That I can find you here. (beat) I want the name of the buyers. I have to stop this.

ERIC: You can't stop it.

TONYA: Yes I can.

ERIC: It's done, Tonya.

TONYA: Nothing is done.

ERIC: There's no turnin' back.

TONYA: I won't let you do this.

ERIC: I didn't have no choice.

TONYA: My memories are not for sale!

ERIC: I didn't sell your memories! The bank took 'em!

TONYA: What?

ERIC: I took out a second mortgage a few years back to pay your mama's medical bills. I woulda done anything to keep her. For however long we could.

TONYA: But you had health insurance.

ERIC: *Had.* (beat) By the time the second course of chemo come around, the coverage ran out. I never thought I couldn't make the payments.

TONYA: We'll fight this. They can't take our home.

ERIC: I fought as hard as I could…for as long as I could. It's done.

TONYA: Why didn't you tell me?

ERIC: How am I supposed to tell you I'm broke?

TONYA: Broke?

ERIC: Started slidin' down when Avondale closed.

TONYA: That was over a year ago. You told me you had another job.

ERIC: I thought I would. Applied at the Bollinger. At Boland. Even tried Austal in Mobile. Nothin'. And the smaller boat shops, they're about all gone now. (beat) I kept up with the house payments as long as I could, went through savin's and retirement.

TONYA: I didn't know.

ERIC: You weren't supposed to know.

TONYA: Of course I was. You're my father.

ERIC: Work all my life to give you and your mama somethin' good and decent. A home. Best I could. Now she's gone. Job's gone. Money's gone.

ERIC sits on a swing.

ERIC: But nobody's takin' this swing-set.

TONYA: Fucking economy.

ERIC: Watch your mouth missy.

TONYA: I'm sorry I haven't been around more. I guess I've been so wrapped up in my own problems it was easy to forget you might have some, too. (beat) We can't just fall apart like this. Mom was always our go-between. When I got in trouble she smoothed things over with you. When you'd be gone testing a new boat for days, she'd make sure I knew how hard you worked. She always made me feel that you loved me.

ERIC: Even when I didn't know how to make you feel it myself. (beat) Seems like she left and took us with her.

PAUSE as TONYA paces, thinking.

TONYA: Move in with me above the restaurant.

ERIC: What?

TONYA: Move in with me above the restaurant.

ERIC: Workin' so hard has made you foolish.

TONYA: I'm serious.

ERIC: It's a bad idea.

TONYA: No. It's not.

ERIC: You think puttin' us under the same roof is gonna slide some kind of closeness on us?

TONYA: How do we know if we don't try?

ERIC: I won't give you another mouth to feed.

TONYA: It doesn't take much for me to fix a little more red beans and rice.

ERIC: I will not have my child taking care of me. I'm supposed take care of you.

TONYA: Then take care of me now.

ERIC: What makes you think I can take care of anything anymore?

TONYA: Maybe neither of us can. Alone. But you can help out in the restaurant for however long I can keep it going. It won't be easy, I know that. But...I need you. Please?

PAUSE

TONYA: It would make mom happy.

PAUSE

ERIC: You still got that little patch of dirt behind the kitchen?

TONYA climbs up the ladder, sits on top of the slide.

TONYA: (nods) Just big enough for this old swing-set. Dad.

ERIC looks up at her.

TONYA slides down the slide.

Lights fade.

END OF PLAY

FREAK OUT

CAST OF CHARACTERS

TAMMY: 50–Stylish–dress is casual designer. Face covered in a mud mask.

KIM: 50–Sporty–dress is relaxed classic sportswear. Always holds cell phone.

BECCA: 50–Funky–dress in gaudy 1980s retro, permed hair streaked with purple and pink stripes.

TIME

Boston, MA. Spring. Present day.

SETTING

A vanity table, vanity chair, a side table. A variety of couture clothing is on the side table. The vanity is covered with various anti-aging lotions, potions, and pills.

SETTING NOTE

Set could be realized with 4ᵗʰ wall as vanity mirror. Set can be simplified to fit minimal staging requirements.

_____

Light drift up in the warm pink hues of rose-colored glasses. TAMMY is seated at the vanity, slathering lotion on her arms and legs. Throughout the beginning of the play she removes mud mask. KIM enters, plops down.

KIM: I don't want to do this.

TAMMY: We have to.

KIM: Maybe she's just holding onto youth while we grow - -

KIM taps on her phone.

TAMMY: I am *not* growing old so don't even say it. (beat) She'll lose her job if she doesn't change. Nothing about her screams luxury spa. We have to confront her. We're her best friends.

KIM: Since junior high.

KIM does a cheerleader movement.

Go Eagles.

TAMMY: Must we? Junior high.

KIM taps on phone. TAMMY looks in mirror, pulls eyebrows up.

KIM: (to phone) Take that!

TAMMY: Are you talking to me or your phone?

KIM: What? Oh. You. As 50th birthday gifts go, confronting her? Not the best.

KIM pounds on her phone as TAMMY continues to take off mud mask.

TAMMY: Not like there's rehab for this.

KIM: Oh hell. Now we're narcs.

TAMMY: Narcs? Junior high and, apparently, a '70s after school special, too.

KIM: Remember those?

TAMMY: I'm not old enough to remember those.

KIM: Uh, yeah, you are. (beat) We're all - -

TAMMY: Don't you say it! I stopped at 39.

KIM: How's that working for you?

TAMMY looks in mirror.

TAMMY: Know what *Boston Financial* had me do this morning? Best places to retire.

KIM: I saw. You weren't exactly smiling through it.

TAMMY: Forget investing, the stock market, economics. Just tell people where to play shuffleboard. (beat – sighs) When did I get this turkey neck? I look like a grandmother.

KIM: You *are* a grandmother.

TAMMY: No one calls me that.

KIM: Right. Sorry. *G-mom.* You sound like a hit man.

TAMMY: Hit *mom.*

KIM: Well G-mom hit mom, at least you get to see them. *This* mom's kids are ten blocks away at B.U. and I still never see them.

TAMMY: You've got us. And we're doing this out of love for Becs so get on-board. Then we'll do a spa afternoon.

KIM: I'm doing sweat yoga. It's the new thing to de-stress. Shania is taking me.

TAMMY: Shania?

KIM taps on phone.

KIM: She's in Derek's stage combat class.

TAMMY: You're hanging out with a 22 year old?

KIM: (nodding) We have a lot in common. (beat as TAMMY stares skeptically) What? Tomorrow we're going to The Dugout.

TAMMY: That dive bar the B.U. kids hang at? Are you also listening to Justin Bieber and trying your hand at Grand Theft Auto?

KIM sheepishly puts phone down.

BECCA: (off-stage) Yo, ho, ho!

KIM: She sounds happy.

TAMMY: She sounds high. (yelling off-stage) We're in the master bedroom.

BECCA bursts through the bedroom door in a flurry of bags and chatter. She's carrying several bags marked 'FREAK OUT - 1980s RETRO'. KIM giggles. TAMMY sighs and wipes the last of the mud mask off her forehead. BECCA excitedly pulls things from her bags as KIM sneaks looks at her phone.

BECCA: Look what I found at Freak Out! Look at this Lame top! Isn't it rad? Oh, oh, oh, and wait. *Look!* A Member's Only jacket in perfect condition! I love this! And I found this never opened packet of pom-pom socks! And, you won't believe this...Gloria Vanderbilt jeans, in my size. Totally bodacious. And look at this hot turquoise Miami Vice T-shirt! Don Johnson is so hot!

TAMMY: Don Johnson doesn't look like that anymore.

BECCA: (BECCA stops her flurry) Tam, what's with the plastic forehead?

TAMMY'S hand shoots to her forehead.

TAMMY: Nothing.

KIM looks up from her phone and peers at TAMMY'S forehead as BECCA continues to empty bags.

KIM: Nothing my ass. What did you do?

BECCA: (pulls out an '80s "Let's Get Physical" headband) I have a great headband for you.

KIM: You didn't. Tammy! You said you were gonna stop.

TAMMY: We're here to help Becca.

BECCA: Oh you will. I have news.

TAMMY: What news?

KIM: Don't change the subject.

TAMMY: Becca *is* the subject.

BECCA: Subject of what?

KIM: Maybe *you* should be the subject.

TAMMY: Okay Miss I-need-to-hang-out-with-20-somethings.

BECCA: (to KIM) You're hanging out with 20-somethings? Why?

TAMMY: Apparently Kim is some kind of friend-cougar.

KIM'S phone suddenly starts crazy-binging. KIM pounds on it.

KIM: No. No! Don't stop playing! Come back on-line!

TAMMY grabs KIM'S phone.

KIM: Hey! Gimme that!

TAMMY holds the phone high as KIM tries to jump for it.

KIM: I need my phone!

TAMMY: (to KIM) You're addicted to this damn phone!

KIM: (to TAMMY) And you're addicted to botox!

BECCA: Does anybody want to try on my Madonna "Like a Virgin" T-shirt?

KIM & TAMMY: (dual dialog) No!

TAMMY throws the phone. KIM scrambles for it.

BECCA: Geez. Take a chill pill.

TAMMY: Chill pill? Becca, it is not 1984!

BECCA: I totally know that.

TAMMY: Totally? Look at yourself! You're not a material girl living in a material world.

TAMMY furiously grabs a Chanel suit and thrusts it at BECCA.

TAMMY: Change. Change! Please. For your own good!

BECCA: What are you talking about?

TAMMY: Chanel. Hermes. Clothes people wear in luxury spas.

BECCA: But that's not me.

TAMMY: Do you know what they're saying about you at the salon?

KIM: Obviously you do since you practically live there.

TAMMY: You've been there three years and they still won't let you see clients. Stefan says he can't keep someone who he can't progress to a client base. You'll lose your job, Becs. Nobody should lose a job. Please.

BECCA: Happy birthday to me. My two best friends think I'm a freak.

PAUSE

KIM: You're not a freak. I told you we shouldn't do this.

BECCA: I completely gross you out.

KIM: No. You don't. Tammy. Tell her.

BECCA: Apparently I do.

TAMMY: I'm sorry. I didn't mean for it to come out that way. I wanted you to…It's just…You are…

BECCA: What?

KIM: *We* are…

TAMMY: Don't make me say it. (pause) 50.

KIM: 50.

BECCA: 50. So what? It's just a number. We're still the same. Aren't we? (beat) Aren't we?

PAUSE

KIM: The only time my kids talk to me is texting or game-play or if I'm at The Dugout pretending I'm 20-something.

TAMMY: *Boston Financial* wants me to retire.

TAMMY crosses to vanity, peers at face, lathers lotions on her face and neck, leaving a streak of white on her neck.

TAMMY: I'm sorry about the whole phone thing.

KIM: Me too.

BECCA: Need I remind you two we had a rad masquerade for Halloween.

KIM: Tomato.

TAMMY: Pirate. Argh!

BECCA: Remember my Boy George? (beat) I bought Freak Out.

TAMMY: You bought - -

BECCA: Freak Out. The most successful retro-80s store in all New England. So here. Change *your* wardrobes.

TAMMY: How did you...

BECCA: Women's Venture Fund. They help with credit for women who can't get loans at stuffy old banks. And I quit the salon. So there.

KIM: Good for you. And Don Johnson is still hot.

KIM puts on the MIAMI VICE T-shirt.

BECCA: You're both helping me outfit the store.

KIM: My kids love 80s wear.

BECCA: You can be there everyday if you want and they can come for the special-kids-of-best-friends-discount.

KIM: Thank you. I love that idea.

BECCA: Your turn. G-mom.

TAMMY: (to BECCA) You're not changing, are you?

BECCA: (shaking head 'no') Are you? I know what you need.

BECCA digs out an 80s power-suit with massive shoulder pads.

BECCA: You can single-handedly bring back the power suit!

KIM: Get on-board.

TAMMY groans.

TAMMY: Is this what 50 looks like?

BECCA: It looks like whatever we want it to.

BECCA dangles suit. TAMMY takes it.

TAMMY: I wonder if *Boston Financial* would go for a segment on investing in the 1980s.

BECCA: If not, you can come work for me. I'll need someone for the money side cuz I'm all about the *fashion*. (beat) Freak Out!

KIM: Bodacious!

TAMMY: Totally rad! Happy birthday, Becs.

KIM: You missed a spot.

KIM reaches over and rubs lotion into TAMMY's neck.

Lights fade to a disco ball sparkling rose-colored lights around the stage, then fade to black.

END OF PLAY

BONES OF HOME

CAST OF CHARACTERS

DILLON: 15 years old, African descent. He has a chip the size of the Super Dome on his shoulders but he has reasons. He speaks with a low-country Louisiana accent.

MIRIAM: 75 years old, Irish descent. She has seen what is left of her life and does not feel it is what she wants.

TIME

10:00 p.m. October 11, 2009.

SETTING

A porch in Provincetown, Massachusetts. A worn-down, tired place which has not seen life in many months. On the porch is a shabby table with one old chair beside it. A bottle of wine, an empty glass, and a bottle of pills are on the table. A small shelf holds a radio.

_____

LIGHTS UP on a deep blue, full-moon night:

A hoodie-clad DILLON slips stealthy onto the porch. He moves to crouch beside a locked window, tries to jimmy it open. After a struggle it pops. As he slowly slides the window up, MIRIAM, carrying a base-ball bat over her head, sneaks up behind him.

MIRIAM: Hey!

> *DILLON spins, the window slams shut on his hand. He falls in pain. MIRIAM wields the bat at him.*

MIRIAM: What are you doing?

DILLON: Don't hit me.

MIRIAM: Why are you trying to sneak into my house?

DILLON: Don't hit me!

> *MIRIAM drops the bat to her side. DILLON starts to rise, she slams the bat against the floor then raises it. He slumps against the house.*

MIRIAM: Don't make me hit you.

DILLON: You gonna call the cops?

MIRIAM: Do I need to?

DILLON: No. I'm just trying to find a place to hide, is all.

MIRIAM: From?

DILLON: None of your business.

MIRIAM: You're on my porch, breaking into my house. I think you made it my business.

DILLON: You're not supposed to be here.

MIRIAM drops the bat to her side.

MIRIAM: (thoughtful) You may be right.

DILLON: I didn't know it was your house. Looks like nobody's been here for months. Figured it be abandoned.

MIRIAM: Neglected. Yes. Abandoned? Soon enough, I suppose. (beat) Who are you hiding from?

DILLON starts to rise to leave. MIRIAM raises bat. DILLON slumps back down.

DILLON: I ain't going back with them. It'd be one thing if they were staying here, here's a little like home. But now, after months, they're leaving and I'm going to *my* home, not theirs.

MIRIAM: Who are they?

DILLON: They're nothing. Nothing to me like I'm nothing to them. Asshat aunt and her asshat Boston family. Only live with 'em cuz I gotta.

MIRIAM: Nothing could be so bad that you have to hide from your family.

DILLON: They ain't my family!

MIRIAM: Be glad you have them.

DILLON: My family be dead. I get shipped up here, not my choice.

MIRIAM: Your family is dead?

DILLON: I don't need to be telling you - -

MIRIAM: You're right. Its just that, well, my family is dead, too.

MIRIAM sits with the bat in her lap.

MIRIAM: Lonely, isn't it? I don't know what to do with myself anymore. Everything is gone. Just gone. Listened to the series yesterday. Alone. Hope for the Red Sox to win the whole thing again but they're down two games to none in the division series. That's gone, too. No need to listen anymore.

DILLON: I hate the Red Sox.

MIRIAM: You're definitely not from around here.

DILLON: I already told you that.

MIRIAM: What team do you root for?

DILLON: Zephyrs. Tigers.

MIRIAM: Louisiana.

DILLON: New Orleans and I'm going home.

MIRIAM: Maybe you can go with your aunt. If you go back and talk to her, I'm sure - -

DILLON: I won't go back there! Hiding out till they give up and head back to Boston without me. Then I'm fixing to take that old truck you got out in the shed.

MIRIAM: Our truck? You can't take our truck.

DILLON: I wasn't exactly gonna ask.

MIRIAM: It was my birthday gift from Jessie. 1969. Same year we bought this place. Our escape, no TV, no phone, just us.

DILLON: Jessie your husband?

MIRIAM: My wife.

DILLON: P'town. I shoulda known.

MIRIAM: We'd explore the old Cape houses with that truck. The Atwood place, Swift-Daley. Used to sneak into Highfield Hall in the '70s when it was falling down from neglect, but there was a beauty in her old bones, a home even as it deteriorated. I'm not sure I like it as much since they fixed her up.

DILLON: Home don't need to be perfect.

MIRIAM rises with bat in one hand, rubs other hand along porch post, hugs it.

MIRIAM: No. But a home needs people to appreciate it, to be a home. And when the people go, sometimes the house dies, too. I just hope it doesn't happen to this place.

DILLON: You going somewhere, too?

MIRIAM: I think it may be time. (beat) You have so much life in you. Mine's gone. It went with Jessie.

DILLON: You dying or something?

MIRIAM: I wish it was that easy. Just die. Then I wouldn't have to think about it.

DILLON: Gonna off yourself?

MIRIAM: Such a poetic way of putting it.

DILLON: That's just stupid.

MIRIAM sits.

MIRIAM: I don't think I can be alone anymore. You're too young to understand.

DILLON: I understand my ma and da didn't have a choice to kill themselves. They drowned. And you're being awful selfish to be making that choice for yourself.

MIRIAM: I'm sorry about your parents.

DILLON: No you ain't. You don't even know me so stop acting like you care. Keeping me here with that bat. Won't gimme your truck. Gonna off yourself? All you are is a old woman being selfish, is all *you* are.

MIRIAM: Maybe…maybe you're right.

DILLON: Yeah.

MIRIAM: What about you?

DILLON: What about me?

MIRIAM: Aren't you being selfish running away?

DILLON: They don't want me.

MIRIAM: They must love you.

DILLON: I didn't wanna come up here. I hate snow. I hate clam chowder. I hate the Red Sox.

MIRIAM: Jessie loved the Sox.

DILLON: I hate my asshat aunt trying to tell me I have to go to school and work in their company. Know what they do?

MIRIAM shakes her head 'no'.

DILLON: Insurance! Insurance wouldn't pay for my house to be re-built and I can't fight them. Been stuck here years with people that don't know me and don't care. Says she wishes…what she wishes is I woulda drowned with 'em so she wouldn't be stuck with me.

MIRIAM: I find that hard to believe - -

DILLON: I won't let you send me back to her! She didn't even try to claim their bodies. Her own sister. Half sister. Always pissed that gramps fucked around and she let me know that too. Didn't even try so they was buried by strangers. Know how I know that? Not from her. I looked it up on the internet. Funeral Association buried them during Hurricane Gustav last year.

MIRIAM: You don't know where they're buried?

DILLON: I gotta find them. I gotta get home and find them or at least be close so I can talk to them and they hear me in the oaks and along the river and in a drafty old Treme cottage where maybe I can hide out as long as I need to feel them.

MIRIAM: How are you going to accomplish that by yourself?

DILLON: I'm old enough. I'm fifteen and I'll do it on my own. Find my own way. First off I'm fixing to drive your truck out of here. First off.

MIRIAM: It's a stick shift.

DILLON: I'll figure it out. I gotta plan.

MIRIAM: Sometimes life throws a curve ball into plans.

DILLON: Already found a room to rent on the Internet.

MIRIAM: That doesn't sound very safe.

DILLON: I ain't stupid. I checked it out. It's in an old Creole cottage across from St. Augustine Church. Just gotta get me to Governor Nicholls.

MIRIAM: Who?

DILLON: It's a street.

MIRIAM: Nicholls was Jessie's last name.

DILLON: So?

MIRIAM: It's just...I haven't heard it in four months, since the funeral. Four months. Two weeks. Five days.

PAUSE

DILLON: Sorry.

PAUSE

MIRIAM: Will you tell me your name?

DILLON: What for? You gonna kill yourself. You don't deserve to know my name.

MIRIAM: I'm Miriam. Now you have to tell me.

DILLON: I don't gotta do nothing. (pause) Dillon.

MIRIAM: You're determined, Dillon.

DILLON: Yeah, you right.

MIRIAM: I understand wanting to be close to someone you love, any way you can make that happen. (beat) I have a favor to ask. Would you stay here, promise not to leave, if I go inside for a minute?

DILLON shrugs his shoulders. MIRIAM places the bat under the table, rises, exits into house. DILLON stares after her, rubs his hand, rises, looks about, turns to leave.

MIRIAM: (off-stage) I have something for you.

DILLON stops. MIRIAM enters carrying a metal bowl with a key in it and a roll of money.

MIRIAM: She's a good truck, always used to start but its been awhile. Jessie's eyes weren't quite what they used to be these last few years. She always saw me, though...I saw her.

DILLON: I get it started.

MIRIAM: The key was rusted to this little metal bowl we kept by the sink along with pin money. A few hundred dollars, not much, but it should get you to New Orleans.

DILLON: Why you doing this?

MIRIAM: Maybe we both need to be home. (pause) Jessie would love that our truck went all the way to a Creole cottage in New Orleans.

DILLON: Bet Jessie would love you fixing this place up, too.

MIRIAM looks around porch, nods. DILLON takes the keys and money from MIRIAM. They stare at each other. DILLON turns, takes a few steps as if to exit, stops, turns back to MIRIAM.

DILLON: You home now. You can't just give up. I'm going home to keep my parents alive, even if they just be in my memories. This place, this house, like my house use to be, hold all your memories. You live, you keep this house alive, keep Jessie alive.

DILLON turns and runs off stage.

MIRIAM: Awfully wise for someone so young.

The sound of a truck trying to turn over is heard. MIRIAM crosses to the wine, pours a glass. The truck finally fires, engine revs. She picks up the pill bottle, stares at it as she runs one hand along the porch rail. The truck's gears grind then it drives off. MIRIAM crosses to the radio, turns it on, listens.

Radio announcer VOICE: (off-stage) With two outs in the ninth, the Soxs look to have the Angels all but silenced in the third game of the division series. Boston needs just one more out to keep their Wild Card playoff run alive and at home in Fenway.

MIRIAM sits with pills in hand.

Lights slowly fade.

END OF PLAY

WHO YOU GOT TO BELIEVE

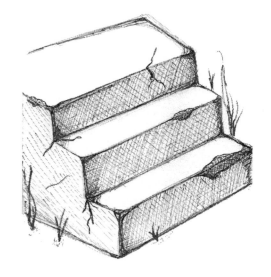

CAST OF CHARACTERS

KATHLEEN: Late 60s. Caucasian.

RAY: Early 60s. African-American.

TIME

A spring night. 2010.

SETTING

New Orleans, LA. A short set of distressed concrete steps surrounded by tall weeds is illuminated at Center Stage. Near the stairs is a pile of moldering trash items including a handkerchief, a dog collar, and old Mardi Gras beads.

———————

Lights drift up in a cool grey-blue. KATHLEEN slowly wanders on stage. She is noticeably disheveled, humming "When the Saints Go Marching In." Thunder is heard in the distance. She stops abruptly at the steps, her humming immediately cuts off. She looks about, bewildered.

KATHLEEN: I's home.

KATHLEEN walks around steps.

Living room.

She turns slowly, shocked and confused at what she does and does not see.

Kitchen? Bedroom?

She crosses to the pile of items, pokes with foot, picks-up an old handkerchief, looks at it, sniffs, trying to recognize it.

Don't smell like me no more. Smells older than me. If that even be possible.

She shakes out the handkerchief, stuffs it into her bosom. She walks around poking the pile and spots something, focuses, her hands coming to her mouth before she picks up the dog collar. She strokes it, shakily touches it to her heart.

Mojo?

She wanders around as if searching.

Mojo!

BEAT. She places the dog collar around her wrist.

You probably long gone, you. I didn't want to leave you. I sorry. I sorry. (Beat) I keep lookin' for you…maybe you comes home to me. That's what I hopes, anyways.

She walks around the pile, picks up several strands of old Mardi Gras beads and places them around her neck.

My place...my home...my steps.

KATHLEEN hums "When the Saints Go Marching In" and looks around, completely lost. RAY, in dirty work clothes and light rain jacket, carrying a well-worn small cooler and a step-ladder, enters. He stops a few feet from KATHLEEN, looks around, following her eyes.

RAY: Where y'at?

He moves closer to her.

Hey chère, I say where y'at? You okay?

He sets his cooler down near her.

It's fixin' to rain, be gettin' dark soon. This ain't no safe place for anybody to be in the dark, alone, not no more, anyway. You got someplace to go? You got people?

KATHLEEN: People gone.

RAY: You got a house? Place to stay, keep you dry?

KATHLEEN: They told me I would...but I don't.

RAY: Who they?

RAY crosses away from KATHLEEN, opens and places step-ladder. He then crosses back to KATHLEEN.

KATHLEEN: All of 'em. They all say it. We gonna take care of you Miss B. Don't you worry now, we give you money and food and we fix your home right fast. I bet they say it to you, too.

RAY: People say lot a things, chère.

KATHLEEN: This...this is my home...what's left of it. Now I own me a nice set a steps.

KATHLEEN sits down on the steps, caressing them.

Don't you think these steps is nice?

RAY: They nice enough, far as steps goes, but not a place for you to be settin' all by yourself.

KATHLEEN: They the best steps in the world. They my steps. This my neighborhood.

RAY: (looks around) Was. One time. Surely was.

KATHLEEN: Is. Is! What you doin' out here in my place, you, anyways, bothering me? I ain't doin' nothin'.

RAY: I volunteer cleaning up. You know, same things we been doin' around here goin' over four years now.

KATHLEEN: I don't know nothin'. They ship me off to some place in Utah. Pretty country out there but what a old Cajun woman like me goin' to do in Utah, alone, with no Mojo to keeps me company? I got no good Andouille to cooks Jambalaya with, no Mormon ever heard of boudin, and they think I's fixin' to be crazy when I asks for a po'boy dressed. No idea what that is, them.

RAY, chuckles. He opens his cooler, takes out a half poor boy sandwich and passes it to KATHLEEN. She looks from it to RAY. She takes a strand of beads from around her neck and hands it to RAY. He nods in appreciation and places it around his neck. KATHLEEN then takes a few bites of the poor boy while looking about.

KATHLEEN: I ain't askin' for much, no, me. I keep goin' all my life bein' one woman maid, one woman cook, one woman dressmaker, I don't like no hand outs, me. I's only had to take care a myself my whole life. Me and Mojo.

She pets the dog collar on her arm then eyes RAY up and down, assessing him.

Never met a man I could stand more than a few years, and I ain't got no use for children. Least that's what I tells myself after the doctor took out my insides. Neighbors all gone now, so just me, alone, wondering why it been four years, goin' *past* four years, why the only thing settin' here now be these concrete steps?

PAUSE—KATHLEEN looks lovingly at steps.

They nice steps, though, don't ya think?

RAY: They nice. But they not a safe place to be, chère, and we gonna be gettin' wet soon. Storm clouds on the way.

KATHLEEN: Storm already rolled in. Rolled out. Rolled over us.

Lights up on step-ladder. She rises, crosses to it and climbs a few rungs.

KATHLEEN: I had me a hurricane protection policy. Cuttin' me a hole in the roof...right about here. Just big enough for my head to fit through so I could breathe. Young coast guard boy flies in a big old helicopter come saves me.

Sounds of helicopter and lapping water are heard. Light shift for flashback.

I hears ya good enough. And I can see ya a little. I'm not blind. (beat) Young man, I's in my attic. My house is flooded. Do I look alright? (beat) This hole not big enough for me. And what about Mojo, here? You got to get us both out, you know.

BEAT as dog barks.

Don't you say Mojo ain't comin' with me, you. I won't have it. He my bébé.

BEAT as dog barks.

Well, if'n you goin' to open it up more, we be stepping back a bit. You best hurry up. Water's risin'.

RAY shakes his head. KATHLEEN descends, crosses to concrete steps and sits: the step-ladder lights, helicopter and water sounds fade out. RAY sits beside her.

RAY: Water's risin'. I tells my Micheleisha when we start to see it oozing in. I want to protect her, get her to safety. Course, once she gets an idea in her head, she like that stubborn old McDonogh oak in City Park. I tells her to come to the attic, that I leave her, leave her and get in the attic alone, if she don't. Just tryin' to get her to listen to reason, ya know? (beat) She saw the men, boys really, taking her bike. Sixty-four year old and she ride that bike everyday. Let 'em have it, I says, and the car too. No. She rush outside; I come down the ladder, almost get to the front door...

Loud sound of single gunshot.

I couldn't protect her.

KATHLEEN: You didn't know what those boys would do, you. Couldn't know.

RAY: Maybe I'll believe that when I see her in the promised land. (beat) Course, she always goin' to be with me long as I stay here. Always my heart. We was together just shy o' forty years. Gawd, I miss that woman, loved her like red beans love rice.

KATHLEEN: I sorry for your loss.

RAY: I sorry for all our loss...and thank you.

RAY rises, offers a hand to help KATHLEEN up.

I best be gettin' on back to my trailer. I can't leave you here, chère, it ain't safe. Can I take you someplace?

KATHLEEN: I told you, I got no place to go.

RAY: How'd you get here?

KATHLEEN: I ain't worked in a hound's age, but I got me a tax refund in the mail. I hide it under my mattress figuring the government gonna want it back. But when they don't, I head to the check casher quicker than a coconut fling from a Zulu float.

RAY chuckles and shakes his head.

So, I got me a Greyhound ticket and then a taxi cab from U.P. Terminal right here to my li'l Alice Court, even though the driver keep sayin' he don't want to be ridin' out here and leavin' me off in the middle of nowhere. I tell him this ain't nowhere, this here be my home.

KATHLEEN looks around, bewildered.

My home. Me and these here steps.

She pats the steps.

They nice steps, solid, strong, they last through anything, these here steps.

RAY: We workin' on gettin' better, sure enough, but still lots a work to be done.

BEAT as RAY looks around, then looks at KATHLEEN.

Didn't you know nothin' been done to your home, yet?

KATHLEEN: How's I suppose to know, way out in Utah? Nothin' on the TV no more. Nobody carin', people think we all right. Nobody tellin' me nothin', 'cept the government peoples and I don't trust them no way, no more. So, I come find out for myself.

RAY: Trick is figuring out who you got to believe.

KATHLEEN: I believed 'em all. And now look where I is.

RAY: Chère, let me takes you on over to my church. We good peoples there, all together like family. Miss Sally, the minister's wife can fix you up some gumbo and we find you a place to stay tonight, someplace safe and dry.

KATHLEEN: No place safe and dry. I gonna stay right here for when they start to build me my house back. I want 'em to know this is my place. My home. My steps.

RAY: You just says you don't trust the government to fix this. Trust *me*. Please. We need to be on our way. What's your name, chère? I'm Ray.

KATHLEEN: You don't need to be knowin' me that much, you. I knows me. I says what I says. I believes what I believes. I knows what I knows. I'm staying home, not leavin' no more.

RAY: But, they ain't gonna be buildin' round these parts for a long time, if ever.

KATHLEEN: Don't you say that! Don't you say that to me, you! They promise they gonna take care of me, they promise and I's gonna hold 'em to it. I is! And I ain't leavin', again. I ain't.

KATHLEEN takes the handkerchief from her bosom and wrings it in her hands.

Now you just go away and leave a old woman alone right here. Why you even stop and talk to me, you? I just mindin' my own business, settin' on my steps, *my steps*, and you comes and bothers me. I ain't doin' nothing' wrong 'cept maybe waitin' for my Mojo. He might come home, ya know. And you, I don't needs you. No, I don't!

PAUSE as RAY ponders his decision to leave her or stay. He crosses to step-ladder, folds it under his arm, crosses back to cooler.

RAY: You surely ain't done nothin' wrong, chère, but I don't want to be leavin' you out here all alone. It ain't right.

PAUSE as RAY looks at KATHLEEN. He picks up his cooler.

RAY: Chère? Please.

KATHLEEN rubs the steps with her old handkerchief. RAY begins to exit. She lies down on the steps and starts humming "When the Saints Go Marching In." He stops. He turns back to look at her, sets the ladder and cooler down, crosses to her, takes off his jacket and places it around her. He sits beside her and sings a verse to "When the Saints Go Marching In" in tune with KATHLEEN's humming.

> We are trav'ling in the footsteps
> Of those who've gone before.
> And we'll all be reunited
> On a new and sunlit shore.

RAY and KATHLEEN hum. As the thunder grows louder.

Lights fade.

END OF PLAY

PROVERBS

CAST OF CHARACTERS

EULALIE: Elderly woman. 1920s humble fashion. Speaks with low-country Louisiana accent.

CLAUDE: Elderly male. Over-sized coat tied with a rope, large worn leather pouch. Speaks with low-country Louisiana accent.

HORSE-MAN: Timeless man dressed in black streetcar driver uniform of the era. No accent. He has the calm of crazy detachment.

TIME

New Orleans, Louisiana. April 29, 1927

SETTING

Interior of horse-drawn streetcar.

SETTING NOTE

Could be realized with chairs only.

———————

The slow rhythmic sound of horses hooves is heard. Cool, blue light fills the stage. EULALIE slumbers on the back bench. HORSE-MAN sits on the front bench holding reins. CLAUDE stands next to HORSE-MAN.

HORSE-MAN: (sing to a slow blues beat)

> With a wicked heart
> he deviseth evil,
> and at all times
> he soweth discord.

CLAUDE: We gots to stop 'em.

HORSE-MAN: You have despised all my counsel and have neglected my reprehensions.

> *HORSE-MAN snaps the reins. CLAUDE limps to EULALIE, shakes her.*

EULALIE: (sleepy) Get away from me. Interruptin' a perfectly peaceful April nap.

CLAUDE: Gots no time to be nappin'. Gots to stop 'em.

EULALIE: (sleepy) Iffin' you gotta stop the streetcar, you go tell the Horse-man.

CLAUDE: Somethin' wrong with that Horse-man.

EULALIE: (sleepy) Then you hop off when I do.

CLAUDE: Where you be doing that you?

EULALIE: (sleepy) Next stop.

CLAUDE: We been on this streetcar since way past *day* sleepin' time. And now the Horse-man pokin' along like a mule on Sunday.

EULALIE: Get away from me fool. It be sunny…

EULALIE looks around with dawning realization.

Where be the sun? Mister Horse-man. You stop this here streetcar right now. I wanna get off.

HORSE-MAN ignores EULALIE, snaps reins.

You not my regular Horse-man. What you done with my regular Horse-man who knows my stops and always has me home for dark? You listenin' to me, fool?

HORSE-MAN: I also will laugh in your destruction and will mock when that shall come to you which you feared.

EULALIE: Don't you be spoutin' Proverbs at me, ole fool. Why you pass my stop? Why it be dark outside?

EULALIE struggles to open window.

Why these here windows all locked up? What kinda Horse-man you be lockin' the windows?

HORSE-MAN: Keeping the paths of justice and guarding the ways of saints.

EULALIE: Damn the saints. Turn this here streetcar around. Today be the day I sees my new grandbaby and my daughter. Ain't seen her since 1915. Since the fallin' out after I make her daddy…after he be dead some dozen years ago. I need to be home.

HORSE-MAN: Be not delighted in the paths of the wicked, neither let the way of evil men please thee.

EULALIE: You don't know me. I ain't got no evils.

CLAUDE: We all gots evils.

EULALIE: I may be havin' evils iffin' you two don't stop bothierin' me and get me off this streetcar, I can tell you that. Ole fools.

HORSE-MAN: (sings to a blues beat)

> A foolish woman
> and clamorous
> and full of allurements
> knowing nothing at all.

EULALIE: Don't you be singin' allurements to me, Mister Horseman. I put my husband in the ground good, and I got no more need for allurements.

CLAUDE: What you mean you put your husband in the ground?

EULALIE: None of your business.

CLAUDE: You kill your husband?

EULALIE: That not what I said and I don't need to be tellin' you.

EULALIE struggles to open one of the windows. It doesn't budge.

CLAUDE: Doors won't budge, neither. We can't be gettin' out but we gots to stop 'em.

EULALIE: Stop sayin' that. I don't gotta be doin' nothin' but gettin' off this streetcar and gettin' home.

CLAUDE: You don't understand. They gonna be blowin' the levee.

EULALIE: The levee? Ain't nobody gonna blow no levee you crazy ole fool. Get away from me.

HORSE-MAN: Make straight the path for thy feet and all thy ways shall be established.

EULALIE: How I suppose to be makin' straight when I stuck on this here streetcar with a crazy ole fool and a proverb singin' Horse-man.

CLAUDE: They gonna blow the levee to stop the floodin'.

EULALIE: Iffin' they do that it *cause* the floodin'.

CLAUDE: Not for their big ole Garden District mansions. Just for *my* home. I goes to the meetin' the other night and asks 'em, I says "Where do they get the power to drown us out, to deprive us of our homes and livin'?" They says if they blow the Caernarvon levee, the river'll stop risin' and we all be saved. *They* all be saved, not me. Ole Jimmy Butler and Mayor O'Keefe in cahoots floodin' *my* home in St. Bernard.

EULALIE: St. Bernard. I live in St. Bernard.

CLAUDE: Not for long you don't iffin' we don't stop 'em. Horseman, you takes this streetcar on over to the rich peoples levee and I stops 'em, I will. Whip the horses and be quick before we ain't gots no home.

EULALIE: I can't be losin' my home. My daughter and grandbaby waitin' there for me.

CLAUDE: I gots the power.

EULALIE: The power?

CLAUDE: To stop 'em.

EULALIE: You think we gots the *power* to stop…this?

 CLAUDE slowly nods.

They got all the power even iffin' we could get off this here streetcar. Even iffin' ole crazy Mister Horse-man be listenin' to me. They *still* got all the power.

CLAUDE: Not if I blow up their levee first.

EULALIE: What you talking 'bout?

CLAUDE: If I blow their levee they too busy savin' their homes to be worryin' 'bout mine.

CLAUDE opens his pouch, shows EULALIE several sticks of dynamite.

EULALIE: You crazy ole fool! You gonna blow us to Pontchartrain with that.

CLAUDE: Maybe I just blow us a way off this here streetcar. Just take one stick at the back door and then we gets home.

EULALIE: One stick? That gonna kill us.

CLAUDE: Iffin' my home be gone, I might as well be dead.

EULALIE: Got to be another way.

HORSE-MAN: (sings to a slow blues beat)

> When the wicked
> man is dead
> there shall be no
> hope any more.

CLAUDE: Can't you see somethin' wrong with Horse-man? He all chalky skin and crazy eyes.

EULALIE: Singin' songs like God.

CLAUDE: Or da devil. He ain't never gonna let us off this here streetcar.

EULALIE: I can't lose my home. Not today. Not with a chance to make things right. (beat) We gots to stop 'em.

CLAUDE removes rope from his coat.

What you thinkin'?

CLAUDE gently lays his pouch of dynamite on the ground, limps slowly to HORSE-MAN, lifts rope over HORSE-MAN'S head.

Don't you be…

Before HORSE-MAN can react, CLAUDE quickly slides the rope around his neck, chokes him. HORSE-MAN goes slack. The slow rhythmic sound of horses hooves stops.

What you done?

CLAUDE: Now I takes this streetcar, go and blows up the rich peoples levee, so they *not* be blowin' mine.

EULALIE: You kilt the Horse-man. They gonna hang you. Take you up to Angola and hang you.

CLAUDE: You too.

EULALIE: I ain't done nothin'.

CLAUDE: You wants to get off this here streetcar much as I did.

EULALIE: To go see my new grandbaby and daughter. To makes things right. Not kill people.

CLAUDE: You my accomplice.

EULALIE: Your what?

CLAUDE: Accomplice. Partner. You helps me.

EULALIE: I didn't do no such thing you crazy ole fool.

CLAUDE: You said yourself we gots to stop 'em.

EULALIE: I didn't mean the Horse-man!

PAUSE

CLAUDE: What you do with your husband?

EULALIE: What?

CLAUDE: You said you buried him.

EULALIE: He was a punchin', hittin' man but that none of your business.

EULALIE starts banging on the windows trying to get out of the streetcar. CLAUDE turns to watch her.

Help! Someone helps me get off this here streetcar. I need to go home!

CLAUDE: I takes you home.

EULALIE: You the devil. The devil for killin' the Horse-man. The devil for temptin' me. Devil!

Unseen by EULALIE and CLAUDE, HORSE-MAN rises up from the dead.

CLAUDE: We all gots evils.

A thunderous boom of exploding dynamite is heard.

EULALIE: *No!* My grandbaby. My daughter.

HORSE-MAN slowly turns with lit match in one hand and stick of dynamite in other. EULALIE and CLAUDE freeze with fear as lights fade to just the glow of the match.

HORSE-MAN: (sings to a slow blues beat)

> But the wicked
> shall be destroyed
> from the earth
> and they that do unjustly,
> shall be taken away from it.

HORSE-MAN blows out match leaving a black stage. The slow rhythmic sounds of horses hooves begin again.

END OF PLAY

One Acts Plays

GIFT OF AN ORANGE

Inspired by Tennessee Williams short fiction piece "Gift of an Apple" written in 1936. Published in *Tennessee Williams Collected Stories*, 1985.

CAST OF CHARACTERS

OSHUN: A woman of Creole descent. She is dark-skinned, plainly clothed, 45 years old. She is scarred by life. OSHUN speaks with a Southern Louisiana accent.

TAUREAN: An African-American man, 19 years old. He is muscular and handsome, looking older than his years. He is dusty from walking. TAUREAN does not have an accent.

JAKE: Burly Caucasian man, 55 years old. His clothing and mannerism reflect a rugged life working on the oil rigs.

TIME

Buras, Louisiana. A hot summer late-afternoon. 2011.

SETTING

A dry, worn-down yet neat yard of a trailer. Two exits: one into the trailer, one to the wood pile and road. A weathered table, two arm chairs, metal washtub, hose are present. A small Voodoo altar is set with a worn New Orleans Saints cap, a photograph of a young man, a knife, and various voodoo items (candles, bells, feathers, colorful cloth, etc.). Honey, herbs, gourds and other natural items are present, for sale. Central to the yard is a lush, blossoming orange tree springing from a small patch of dark, rich earth circled by stones. It is a sharp contrast to the rest of the worn-down yard.

INSTRUMENTATION

A Jembe drum can be used to personify Oshun's desires. A flute can be used to personify Taurean's emotions. A chime can be used to represent the magic.

Scene One

Lights drift up in the bright midday sun. Faint birdsong is heard. OSHUN, humming to a blues beat dances in from the trailer carrying a wooden bowl, a straight pin, a glass of water. She gathers herbs, spices and an orange from the tree. She is barefoot, wearing a light cotton dress with a waist-pocket.

OSHUN: (sings)

> I'm a voodoo woman since I been born,
> Mother nature's bounty, the pact I've sworn,
> Loas be my guides to the sky and earth,
> I call down the spirits: joy, pain, rebirth.

She continues to hum tune.

OSHUN crosses to table with items. She breathes on the herbs, places all items in the bowl, pricks her finger, lets the blood drip into the water, mixes. She crosses, with bowl, to tree and sprin-

kles the ingredients at the base. She begins to dance about the tree in wild abandon.

OSHUN: Mother Earth, while I am yet alive, it upon you I put my trust. Mother Earth who receives my body, we are addressin' you, and you will understand. With these words and this potion I call on the fruit of the land, bring love to me, place it in my hand to heal my heart, my body so grand.

She dances then plucks an orange from tree, crosses to Saints hat, picks it up, breathes it in, lovingly pets hat.

OSHUN: (speaks to herself, smiles sadly) How you like oranges, my bébé boy. One thing always grow out here, no matter what. Course, I help it along. Yes I do.

OSHUN puts hat back, rips open the orange and eats. TAUREAN enters dressed in jeans, T-shirt and sneakers, carrying a worn backpack. OSHUN watches him. He hungrily eyes the items in the yard, sees the tree and stops. After a moment he starts to walk away.

OSHUN: (smoothes the front of her dress) You want to buy somethin', you?

TAUREAN stops.

TAUREAN: I don't have any money.

OSHUN: Huh. You *and* me. That why I'm sellin' my…things. (beat) C'mon over here, maybe you find somethin' you like.

TAUREAN: I just need something to eat.

OSHUN: Been a might since you had somethin' good to eat?

TAUREAN nods.

OSHUN: Where you walkin' from, you?

TAUREAN: Up New Orleans way.

OSHUN: You walk sixty miles into the bayou?

TAUREAN: Mostly. Hitched some but didn't have any money to give for gas and didn't want to ride with drunks. Besides I can take care of myself.

OSHUN: What you doin' up there, you?

TAUREAN: Looking for a job.

OSHUN: No money. I say you didn't find one.

TAUREAN: I will. Have to.

OSHUN: C'mon over here. I give you somethin'.

TAUREAN: No. Thanks.

OSHUN: Look to me like you might need a few things, including that job.

TAUREAN: You got one?

OSHUN: I'll think on it. Come. Sit. Be a might before you see another body along this here road. C'mon. I'm not a gator, I won't bite.

TAUREAN backs up a step.

OSHUN: Didn't your mama teach you manners?

TAUREAN: (defensively) You don't know anything about my mama.

OSHUN: I only meant I'm invitin' you to my table. Come on now, sit on down.

TAUREAN: I don't have time to hang around here.

OSHUN: Well then, I guess I best be quick about…feedin' you.

OSHUN motions him to the table. He hesitates then slowly crosses and sits.

OSHUN: That more like it.

PAUSE as she stares at him.

TAUREAN: I was hoping to find more people out this way.

OSHUN: Me, too. (beat) It's a quiet place but it's comin' alive again. There be peoples wander back, not as many like before.

TAUREAN: Nothing like before. (beat) I need to find work, maybe a fishing boat.

OSHUN: Fishin' jumpin' a might again but still a ways to go.

TAUREAN: I'll find something. Take care of myself. Maybe try my hand at rough necking on the oil rigs. (beat) Need to be on my way soon and see what's out there.

OSHUN: Rough neckin' on the rigs? How old you be, you?

TAUREAN: Old enough.

OSHUN reaches across the table, runs a hand down his cheek. He backs his face away. She smiles.

OSHUN: You got soft skin, but I 'spect you are...old enough. Maybe just, though.

OSHUN takes bowl, crosses to the orange tree.

OSHUN: Don't matter much. No fishin' boats hirin' right now. Oil work still about the new rigs buildin' up. That's good for me, more people comin' out this way, be wantin' my advice and goods, but they ain't hirin'.

TAUREAN: You give advice?

OSHUN: I do.

TAUREAN: Like Dear Abby?

OSHUN: Not quite. Mine come with cards and cat bones.

TAUREAN: What?

OSHUN: You born here abouts?

TAUREAN: Yeah.

OSHUN rips a few oranges, crosses back to table.

OSHUN: Then don't you go actin' dumb. You know what a woman fixin' to do with cards and cat bones.

TAUREAN: I heard stories. I never seen - -

OSHUN: You wanna see from me?

TAUREAN shrugs his shoulders.

OSHUN: (chuckles) Mmm-hmmm.

PAUSE.

TAUREAN: Are you any good with advice?

OSHUN: I am.

TAUREAN: And other stuff?

OSHUN walks around TAUREAN, smiles.

OSHUN: I'm good with everythin'. What you want, you?

TAUREAN: I mean other stuff with cards and bones, maybe connecting people.

OSHUN: What people you want connection with, you?

TAUREAN rises, crosses away from her, hugs himself.

OSHUN: Most my advice sought by folks what have sadness in their lives. You too vibrant for that.

TAUREAN: (turns to face the orange tree) I wish that were true.

OSHUN: They look good, no?

TAUREAN: They look perfect. I don't think I've ever seen oranges quite like them.

OSHUN: Stay with me a bit. I give you one.

TAUREAN: I'm heading on down the road, see what I can find.

OSHUN: I already told you, no work down there.

TAUREAN: Don't seem to be any here, either.

OSHUN: I could find lots of things to keep you here. (beat) I tell you what, you see that woodpile? It needs stackin'. You do it. I pay you.

TAUREAN: With more than an orange?

OSHUN: Once you nibble on something so juicy, you might not want anything else, chère.

TAUREAN: I'll need more.

OSHUN: Maybe I'm fixin' to give you more.

TAUREAN: I don't know - -

OSHUN: Yes, you do. A good day of work might just bring pleasure to both of us.

> *OSHUN motions for TAUREAN to exit to woodpile: he does as she watches him. Lights fade.*

Scene Two

Lights up: afternoon sun begins to slip away. OSHUN stands by table, wringing out TAUREAN'S damp shirt.

OSHUN: (sings)

> I'm a voodoo woman, cast your love to me
> All else disappear, I be what you need
> Call down the spirits, twine an ache with you

My charms brew in your body, I be your only view

TAUREAN enters, shirtless, wet with sweat, crosses around the orange tree, looking at it.

OSHUN: I washed it out a bit but don't have no dryer. Hang it over the chair, take a short time in this heat.

TAUREAN: I can wear it wet.

OSHUN: It'll stick to you. No comfort there.

TAUREAN: Who says I'm looking for comfort?

OSHUN snaps out the shirt, hangs it over a chair.

OSHUN: You been stackin' a few hours. The rest of the wood can wait and I owe you an orange.

TAUREAN: I've been wondering about these oranges. You notice this tree the only thing all blooming in your yard?

OSHUN takes a knife from her pocket.

TAUREAN: It's like nothing else alive out here except these oranges.

OSHUN: Trust me, chère, I'm alive. Very much alive.

TAUREAN: Nothing is *growing* except this orange tree. Why is that?

OSHUN shrugs, takes an orange from the bowl on the table.

OSHUN: Why question it? Just come over and enjoy.

TAUREAN: It don't feel right. I feel - -

OSHUN: *I* feel.

TAUREAN: What?

OSHUN: You come over here now and I'll pay you.

TAUREAN: I'm just gonna take my shirt and go.

OSHUN: Go to what, you?

TAUREAN: Go further south.

OSHUN: I didn't say where. I say to what.

TAUREAN: To a job. Maybe people down there.

OSHUN: I'm not people?

TAUREAN: I'm *not* curious about you.

> *OSHUN laughs, cuts orange with knife, sniffs deeply as the aroma fills the air. TAUREAN sniffs.*

OSHUN: Smell even better than they look, no?

TAUREAN: I gotta go. I just need my shirt.

> *OSHUN takes a slice of orange, crushes it. TAUREAN begins to cross to his shirt but she cuts him off, brings the orange to his mouth. He tries to move around her but she places one hand on his chest stopping him.*

OSHUN: Bite. Take it. I give them somethin' special.

TAUREAN: I don't need nothing special from you or anyone else. I can take care of myself.

> *She bites the orange slice, juice runs down her fingers.*

OSHUN: Just a taste.

> *She slides the hand from his chest to caress his cheek. He tries to move away.*

TAUREAN: Get away from me.

OSHUN: I give you work and this how you pay me, you?

TAUREAN: *You* were supposed to pay *me*. Guess not, huh?

OSHUN: One bite and I will.

TAUREAN: One bite?

OSHUN: If that's all you want.

She tickles his lips with the orange, his lips part.

OSHUN: (sings)

> I'm a voodoo woman

She smiles and feeds him.

OSHUN: Good. Yes?

TAUREAN: Tastes like an orange. Don't look like you're gonna give me what I need.

OSHUN: (sings)

> Cast your love to me

TAUREAN: I'm going.

TAUREAN tries to move around OSHUN, she counters his movements, stopping him.

OSHUN: One more bite.

TAUREAN: You said only one.

OSHUN: You need more.

TAUREAN: I don't think so.

TAUREAN pulls away from OSHUN, picks up his shirt, starts to exit.

OSHUN: (sings)

> All else disappear.

(stops singing) Take this for the road. It already cut up.

TAUREAN: I'm fine.

OSHUN: All I ask is you take the orange.

TAUREAN: That all?

OSHUN gives TAUREAN the orange slices. He turns to exit, takes a slice, eats it.

OSHUN: (sings)

> All else disappear,
> I be what you need.
> What you need.
> What you need.

TAUREAN stops.

TAUREAN: It tastes…different. Sweeter. Deeper.

OSHUN: More?

TAUREAN: (growing weak) I said only one…

OSHUN: That all you want, you? Really? (sings)

> Call down the spirits, twine an ache with you.

TAUREAN: (weaker) I don't…I don't know.

OSHUN: More.

TAUREAN turns to OSHUN. He swoons. She guides him back to the chair: he does not resist. She sits on the chair arm, rips open another orange, feeds him. TAUREAN looks up at her.

TAUREAN: I never tasted an orange as good as this.

OSHUN: (touches his face and hair) Maybe you was just that hungry. I am. It gets lonely now out here, middle of nowhere. It's nice to have someone kind and strong around.

TAUREAN: I can be kind and strong.

OSHUN: I know. Trust me.

TAUREAN: I do.

OSHUN leans into TAUREAN, runs a finger wiping juice from his face. She smiles.

OSHUN: Now, yes. I think now you will stay with me. (singing)

> My charms brew in your body, I be your only view. Your only view.

OSHUN kisses TAUREAN passionately. JAKE enters.

JAKE: Well, ain't this a pretty sight.

OSHUN rises.

TAUREAN: May I have another orange, please?

JAKE: Go ahead, give him another.

OSHUN: In a bit.

TAUREAN: I never tasted oranges as good as these.

JAKE: Yeah, you right. These the best damned oranges in the world. Who's the kid?

TAUREAN: I'm not a kid.

OSHUN: No, you're not.

JAKE: What's he doing here?

OSHUN: He lookin' for work, was wondering' about the oil rigs- -

JAKE: I just come off a seven week stretch getting' one of the new rigs up and runnin'. All veteran riggers. We ain't hirin'.

OSHUN: I told him so. I give him some work here.

JAKE: Yeah? What else you givin' him?

OSHUN crosses to JAKE.

OSHUN: I save that for you.

JAKE: You hear that, kid? She means I'm her lover. Best damn lover she ever did have.

OSHUN: You think so?

JAKE: (laughs) I know so, my li'l witchy woman.

JAKE grabs OSHUN, pulls her into a rough hug, smells her hair, nibbles her neck.

JAKE: The kid needs to leave. Run along.

TAUREAN rises abruptly, pushing his chair back forcefully: it tips over.

TAUREAN: I'm not a kid!

OSHUN: He's old enough.

JAKE: Ha. When did you start 'em so young?

TAUREAN takes a few steps towards JAKE and OSHUN.

TAUREAN: If you don't let her go you're gonna find out how young I am.

JAKE: Kid, this is my grabbin' on time so you'll understand if I ain't about to be lettin' go. Witchy woman here about the only thing in thirty miles worth a trip. (beat) And she got the best oranges I ever did taste.

OSHUN: You mean my tree?

JAKE: (laughs lustily) I mean you and your tree, darlin'.

TAUREAN paces.

OSHUN: You a handful.

JAKE: You love my hands.

OSHUN: They alright.

JAKE: I'm missin' your hands, your massages. You a comfort for these weary bones.

OSHUN: What be weary, you?

JAKE: Ha! Not that bone. Definitely not that. Chère, I been thinkin' about you for almost two months. Get me through some long nights in the middle of the Gulf.

OSHUN: Sometimes you a charmer.

JAKE: Right now I'm an impatient charmer. How 'bout we stop jawin', get rid of the kid, and you get in that bed with me.

JAKE grabs at OSHUN'S breast. She pushes his hand away.

OSHUN: We got time for that later. You come back in a few days.

JAKE: Fuck a few days. I'm out for three weeks and I'm ready now.

OSHUN: I'm not. You go now.

JAKE: I don't think so. Get the fuck outta here, kid, so I can take witchy woman inside and show her how a real man cast a spell, if ya know what I mean. Cuz if you're thinkin' you can make it happen, trust me, she's way out of your league.

TAUREAN stops pacing.

TAUREAN: Leave her alone.

JAKE: You're a feisty crawdad, ain't ya?

TAUREAN: She said no.

JAKE: Kid, I'm lookin' to be a lover today, not a fighter. But don't push it.

TAUREAN: Maybe she don't need you anymore.

JAKE: That it, woman? You don't need me?

OSHUN: I need different things, different peoples, different times.

JAKE: Yeah? Guess what I need? Scram kid.

TAUREAN: You scram, old man!

JAKE: I been tryin' to nice about this, kid but you're just not *gettin' it*.

JAKE pushes OSHUN aside and lunges at TAUREAN who sidesteps. JAKE falls, rises. They fight.

OSHUN: (yelling) Stop! Jake! You leave! Go!

The men ignore her, fighting escalates. She grabs herbs, dried flowers, and an orange off the tree. JAKE pushes TAUREAN back and grabs the knife on the table. They face-off. OSHUN steps towards them.

JAKE: (to OSHUN) What are you doin' with those things?

OSHUN stops.

OSHUN: Why don't we all calm down?

JAKE: I know all about you. You and that name of yours. Some voodoo love African Venus. I see you, when you think I'm sleeping. At that table of yours. Prayin'. Chantin'. Whatever the fuck you doin'. You ain't none of that. What we got here is you and me just passing the hours, feeding each other's needs.

OSHUN: That all you think?

JAKE: Not one fucking thing more. And now you think you're tryin' that voodoo shit on me?

OSHUN: Just. Like. Always.

JAKE: Bullshit. You and I, we're one in the same. Come in like a *flood* and take *what* we want. *When* we want.

OSHUN: No.

JAKE: You keep tellin' yourself that, darlin'.

JAKE slashes with the knife trying to strike TAUREAN who falls. OSHUN crushes the orange, herbs and flowers, and waves them about.

OSHUN: (chants at JAKE) I banish all forces not in harmony with me. We are addressin' you.

JAKE: You hear that kid, she thinks she's gonna hex me. Witch.

OSHUN: We are addressin' you.

JAKE: (growing weak) Not me. Not me.

OSHUN: Banish all forces hostile.

JAKE gets wobbly.

JAKE: (weaker) It's not gonna work.

OSHUN: It already is. You will understand.

JAKE drops the knife. TAUREAN starts to rise but OSHUN motions for him to stay down.

OSHUN: Breathe.

JAKE takes a deep breath. OSHUN motions for him to come to her: he does. JAKE gently leans into her and nuzzles. He is docile now, almost childlike.

JAKE: You smell delicious. Like honey. I need honey.

OSHUN: I know and didn't I always give you what you needed.

OSHUN gets a basket, drops in the orange crush, puts in a jar of honey, hands it to JAKE. He takes a large wad of cash from his pocket, hands it to her. She gently urges him away from her. He exits.

TAUREAN: What just happened?

OSHUN: He calmed down, is all.

TAUREAN: I never seen anything...what the hell are you?

OSHUN: You already know the answer to that.

OSHUN puts the money on her voodoo altar. TAUREAN rises. The sun continues to set.

TAUREAN: Will he come back?

OSHUN: (with conviction) I don't want him back.

TAUREAN: What did you do to him?

OSHUN: Nature.

TAUREAN: I don't understand.

OSHUN: I know.

TAUREAN: He's your lover?

OSHUN crosses to TAUREAN.

OSHUN: No. A lover is someone I want to share my heart with. Someone kind and strong. That's not what he was. He was just a necessity. The others, too.

TAUREAN: There are others?

OSHUN nods.

TAUREAN: Why?

OSHUN: They bring me things.

TAUREAN: Money. You make them bring you money.

OSHUN: That's not a bad thing. I buy this trailer. Food. My things. I live simple, sell what I can, advise when I can. After the storm I only gots me to rely on, take care of. Everything... everyone in my heart gone so (beat) let's just say I have many visitors what helps pass the hours. And, nature, she makes them easier to control. Some are gentle. Some just want talk. Others? Sometimes a warm body be good, even if it be a lie.

TAUREAN: You said you was lonely.

OSHUN: Havin' visitors got nothin' to do with bein' lonely.

PAUSE

TAUREAN: You asked if I wanted to know how you...make things special. I do need to know.

OSHUN: You sure, you?

TAUREAN nods.

OSHUN: Why it so important to you?

TAUREAN: There's someone I need to connect with.

OSHUN: What's your name?

TAUREAN: Taurean.

OSHUN: Taurean? Why I know that name?

TAUREAN: Used to play football for the Belle Chase Cardinals. Best running back they ever had. Got my name in the Picayune. Scouts came looking my junior year but...then it all fell apart. Football. Grades. All gone. I just managed to graduate. Two years ago.

OSHUN: Two years? That mean you? (beat) *Nineteen.* You can't be only nineteen. You look - -

TAUREAN: Older.

OSHUN: How that possible? *Nineteen.*

PAUSE. OSHUN is lost in thought before TAUREAN breaks the silence.

TAUREAN: Two years. Seems like a lifetime.

OSHUN: A lifetime. A lifetime.

TAUREAN: I wouldn't change it, you know. What I did those last few years. Not for anything. (beat) But Mama still died. Cancer. I hate that she had to see this emptiness before she passed. See our memories washed away.

OSHUN: You be young to know this much hurt. So young.

TAUREAN: I'm not a kid.

OSHUN: You got family, you?

TAUREAN: Just mama. Took care of her till the end.

OSHUN: Through her pains?

TAUREAN nods.

OSHUN: Through her loneliness?

TAUREAN: Don't know that she was lonely.

OSHUN: She was. And you a good...*young* man. You already connect with your mama, you.

TAUREAN: How do I do that?

OSHUN: You talk to her even now?

TAUREAN: Every day.

OSHUN: Then you feel her in your heart.

TAUREAN nods.

OSHUN: Trust me.

TAUREAN: I do.

OSHUN: She's around, always. You not ever be lonely.

TAUREAN: You don't have to be lonely, either.

OSHUN looks at him thoughtfully, picks up the bowl of oranges, crosses to the tree, leaves bowl there.

TAUREAN: You coming back here with those?

OSHUN picks up Saints hat, brushes a strand of hair from TAUREAN'S eyes, puts hat on his head.

TAUREAN: I don't want a hat.

TAUREAN takes hat off, hands it to OSHUN. She places it in her pocket. He encircles her with his arms, nuzzling into her breasts.

TAUREAN: I want you.

She lingers a moment before disentangling herself. He follows after her.

TAUREAN: I'll stay with you and work hard. And it won't be a lie.

OSHUN: Bring me love?

TAUREAN: I'll bring you anything.

TAUREAN kisses her passionately. She pushes him and crosses away.

OSHUN: I suppose football star who takes care of his mama through her pains be kind and strong. Like my boy, Rada.

TAUREAN: Your boy?

OSHUN: (nods) Nineteen years old.

TAUREAN: My age.

OSHUN: Played football for LSU And he loved him his Saints. (beat) The storm hit just before he was headin' back to school for his second year. (pause) The water claimed him. (beat) It was too fast. We was too slow. I went in after him, next thing I remember is that hospital in Baton Rouge and his coach standin' over me. Stayed up there a while, healin'…my body, but I had to come back. (beat) Miss him everyday but he still my heart and I talk to him even now.

TAUREAN: I'm sorry.

OSHUN nods.

OSHUN: You finish the woodpile, now, you?

TAUREAN: Anything you want.

OSHUN smiles at him, pats his arm. TAUREAN exits to the woodpile. Lights fade.

Scene Three

Lights come up on night. A towel is hung over a chair. TAUREAN is asleep under the orange tree. OSHUN kneels beside him, strokes his hair as she very slowly sings.

OSHUN: (sings)

> A serpent on my shoulder
> Twine an ache with you,
> My charms, your desires,
> Make intoxicating brew.

> *PAUSE*

> Twine an ache with you,

> *PAUSE*

> Make intoxicating brew.

OSHUN: My charms. Your desires. You could bring me love. But what the cost be?

> *OSHUN rises, gathers herbs and jars in yard, crosses back to TAUREAN as she tries to convince herself of what she already knows.*

OSHUN: Water as child of earth, why you bring this man...this *boy* to me? Sometime your will be cruel.

> *OSHUN softly kisses TAUREAN, crosses to hose, puts it in tub, turns it on. Running water is heard.*

OSHUN: Give me strength not to take, but to give. Give.

> *OSHUN places herbs and other ingredients into the water, hikes up her skirt and steps into the tub, swirling in the water.*

OSHUN: Water as child of earth, it upon you I must put my trust. Water who cleanse my body, we are addressin' you and you will understand. I ask you to bring love for my body, my heart and now I ask to see your ways. He a fine boy, like my Rada. So young. *Too* young. If it your will, give

85

me strength to transfer the spell into the water and make it sleep. No harm will come from the cancellin' of this here spell. No further power shall it have.

OSHUN steps out of water, scooping some into a small wooden bowl. She crosses to the sleeping TAUREAN and rubs his arms with the water. He stirs, opening his eyes.

TAUREAN: (groggy) Where am I?

OSHUN: Been sleepin' under the orange tree about an hour.

TAUREAN: What are you doing?

OSHUN: Wiping sweat from you. You work hard today.

TAUREAN: (sits up) I ate oranges.

OSHUN: And you stack the wood.

TAUREAN: And I fought an old man.

OSHUN: Me too. An old man and his ways.

PAUSE as TAUREAN snuggles next to OSHUN.

OSHUN: I made a bath for you.

TAUREAN: I don't want a bath.

OSHUN: (sniffs) You do, trust me.

TAUREAN sniffs under his arms and laughs.

TAUREAN: Ripe?

OSHUN: All young men get ripe when they work hard. Have you ever done bathin' outside, you?

TAUREAN: No. But if you bathe with me...

OSHUN: I give it somethin' special. Outside bathin' a joyful experience. My Rada did almost everyday, even in the storms. I used to yell to him come in before lightening strike, but he just laugh at his old mama.

OSHUN guides TAUREAN to the metal tub. She begins to undress him, lifting the T-shirt over his head.

TAUREAN: You're not old.

She runs her hands down his chest, stopping at his jean buttons

OSHUN: You should do this yourself bébé.

He moves his hands to hers, looks at her with passion, caresses her face and arms.

TAUREAN: I want you to.

OSHUN runs her hand down his cheek, shakes her head, then steps back, turns off hose, crosses away from him, her back to him. TAUREAN removes his shoes, socks.

TAUREAN: You never told me your name.

OSHUN: I know.

TAUREAN: Tell me.

OSHUN: Why it important? You leave soon, bébé.

TAUREAN: I want to stay.

OSHUN: (speaks to herself) But I must be strong. Let you leave.

TAUREAN: What's in the water? It smells good, like...(sniffs) mama's garden.

TAUREAN removes his pants and briefs. He is naked.

OSHUN: Rosemary oil, angelica, benzoin from the tree bark.

TAUREAN: Why all that stuff?

OSHUN: It something I do when I need be changin' something I did.

TAUREAN: What?

OSHUN: My oranges, they soothin', sometimes more powerful than other times. They about connection. Could be lovers. Pleasure. Be family. Peace. Heart. You took it all in, and it change you. And now I change you back.

TAUREAN: I like where I am now. With you.

OSHUN: Part of me wishes I could keep you.

TAUREAN: You can. I don't want to change.

OSHUN: No matter, bébé.

TAUREAN: It does matter.

OSHUN: Get in the bath. It'll make you feel good.

TAUREAN: *You* make me feel good.

> *TAUREAN embraces OSHUN from behind and kisses her neck. He pulls her back to the bath, slides into it, bringing her with him.*

TAUREAN: This feels real. Good.

OSHUN: It feels good. But what you feel is…is my doin'. It nature and no further power shall it be havin'.

TAUREAN: I don't care what it is.

OSHUN: I care. I release it. Must have strength to release you.

TAUREAN: No release. I'll do anything. Wear that Saints' hat even. Whenever you want, for as long as you want.

> *OSHUN abruptly rises from the tub. TAUREAN holds out his hands to her.*

OSHUN: Rada's hat?

> *OSHUN shakes head 'no'.*

TAUREAN: Want you.

OSHUN: No!

TAUREAN: I will love you.

OSHUN: I can't have this love.

TAUREAN: You wanted me. I know you did. I felt it when you first kissed me. Why are you fighting this now?

OSHUN: The others, *they* come to *me* and I bind them to me with my oranges. You, you *fought* me and I thought you might ease the loneliness. Might be real. But you not be real. You be *young. Nineteen.* I can *not...flood* over you and take what I needs. I must *give.* Must give you the life my Rada never had the chance to be livin'.

TAUREAN: I want to live with you. I don't understand.

OSHUN: You no need to. Trust me. Please. Feel the water. Feel it work into you. Feel it release you.

TAUREAN: Don't want release.

OSHUN: Do it feel good?

TAUREAN: (feeling release) Yes.

OSHUN pours water over TAUREAN.

OSHUN: Do you still want to stay, you?

TAUREAN: (feeling release) I don't know.

OSHUN: No harm may come from makin' it sleep. Please, gives me strength, make it sleep.

TAUREAN: (feeling more release) Sleep.

OSHUN: No further power shall it have.

She rubs water on him.

What you want now, bébé?

TAUREAN: (feeling more release) Don't know.

OSHUN: I see your ways, water as child of earth. (beat) I thinks you do. Say it. Say it.

TAUREAN: I need...to move on.

OSHUN rises, crosses to towel.

OSHUN: Need a powerful word.

TAUREAN: So is pain and lonely.

OSHUN: Like your mama had.

TAUREAN: And you. (beat) And me.

OSHUN: You can know those feelin's so young.

TAUREAN: I grew up fast.

OSHUN: You did. (beat) I miss people. Kind people. Real people.

PAUSE

OSHUN: Time to get out.

TAUREAN: Time to get out.

TAUREAN gets out of the tub. OSHUN hands him a towel then crosses away from him. He dries himself, dresses.

TAUREAN: I'm not sure I understand what happened today.

OSHUN: You did everythin' right, bébé.

TAUREAN: I can take care of myself.

OSHUN: You been doin' that for two years. You needs more now. Do you still trust me? Trust Oshun?

TAUREAN: (nods) Oshun.

OSHUN crosses to altar, takes JAKE'S money, crosses to TAUREAN.

OSHUN: I want to give you this. It gets you to Baton Rouge.

TAUREAN: Baton Rouge?

OSHUN: Go see Coach Morris at LSU. He be helpin' you get settled. I tells him you a good boy, you.

TAUREAN: I'm old enough.

OSHUN: I 'spect you are old enough.

TAUREAN: Can I take some oranges?

OSHUN shakes her head 'no'.

TAUREAN: Will you be okay?

OSHUN: I be okay. (pause) It good you be here today, you.

TAUREAN: Oshun. Thank you for - -

OSHUN: No need to thank me bébé. It was upon you I put my trust.

TAUREAN picks up his backpack and slowly exits. OSHUN crosses to the altar and places the Saints hat on it. She crosses to tub, takes a bowlful of water, crosses to orange tree, and pours it around the base.

OSHUN: Water as child of earth, with these words and this potion I *release* the fruit of the land. No further power shall it have. I takes no more. I *give*. Find love myself. Put it in my own hand.

OSHUN sings.

> I'm a voodoo woman since I been born,
> Mother Nature's bounty, the pact I've sworn,
> Now I find my own way with the sky and earth,
> I use my giving strengths! Joy! Change! Rebirth!

OSHUN dances with abandon.

Lights fade.

END OF PLAY

ANOTHER AUGUST

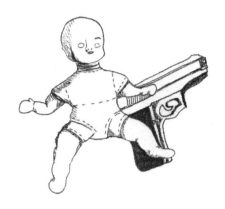

CAST OF CHARACTERS

Jimmy: 18 years old. Pulsing with energy.

Ruby: 18 years old. A gentle soul.

Prentiss: 58 years old. Cautious. Heavy set.

CHARACTER NOTES

All characters are African-American, dressed in grey cotton pants and grey pocket T-shirts, similar to hospital scrubs.

TIME

August 29, 2008

SETTING

Three long wooden boxes arranged neatly on the floor. Upstage a table holds an empty dusty coffee pot, a radio: underneath are file boxes with yearly dates 2005, 2006, 2007, 2008. A large calendar on the table or hung: showing date August 29, 2008.

In darkness, a RADIO ANNOUNCER is heard. As he speaks, the lights slowly up in a grey haze. RUBY, wrapped in a sheet covering her head and body, sits on one of the wooden boxes. She holds a baby doll under the sheet. PRENTISS on floor pulling newspapers and reports from box marked '2008.' JIMMY sits on the table, watching PRENTISS.

RADIO ANNOUNCER: August 29, 2008. The National Hurricane Center is calling for Hurricane Gustav to make landfall late Monday near Houma as a category three with winds up to 130 miles per hour. Detailed information on New Orleans' latest preparations, evacuation plans and more will be...

JIMMY plays with radio knobs then shuts off radio, slips off table, inches closer to PRENTISS who doesn't see him. RUBY sees JIMMY who quickly turns, faces the calendar and punches it.

JIMMY: Still.

RUBY: Still, what?

JIMMY: What you mean, what? You gone stupid or something, girl? Another August. Another hurricane on the way and we're *still here.*

PRENTISS: Can't get out.

RUBY: Can't have another hurricane come through and flood over us again.

JIMMY: Maybe you can take those boxes Blue always dug into, stack 'em up and climb - -

PRENTISS: To what?

JIMMY: Maybe a (sings the title of a song like a "Stairway to Heaven").

Ha!

RUBY: Leave him alone.

JIMMY: Well, ain't you just the princess.

Picks up empty coffee pot, takes deep breath.

JIMMY: Ahhh, the sweet smell of chicory in the morning.

RUBY: The pot is empty.

JIMMY: Stop mumbling. Take that sheet off your head.

RUBY: I don't want to.

JIMMY: What'd you mean you don't want to?

RUBY: Maybe I'm cold.

JIMMY: (sarcastically) Yeah, like you can feel the cold.

RUBY: (sarcastically) Like you can smell coffee.

JIMMY whips sheet off RUBY who is holding the baby doll.

JIMMY: You and that damned doll.

RUBY: My baby.

JIMMY: You ain't got no baby.

RUBY: You don't know - -

JIMMY: You all addicted to that doll and it ain't real.

PRENTISS: What are you addicted to?

JIMMY: You addicted to them boxes, Blue. Every time a new one shows up outta some limbo under that table, you get all obsessed and start diggin'. I been tellin' you for three years no good come outta it.

JIMMY kicks file boxes.

RUBY: You're such a child. God.

JIMMY: God got nothin' to do with this. Haven't you figured that out by now?

PRENTISS rises, crosses to a wooden box with '2008' file box, sits, digs in box.

RUBY: (rocking on wooden box with doll) We have to hope that God gonna help get us home. With our families.

JIMMY: Ruby, you're delusional. Holding onto that doll like it's gonna talk at you. 'Sides, my mama always tell me God workin' good. If anything, this is evil. We're practically in a morgue, for hell's sake.

RUBY: You think I don't know that?

JIMMY: What we done to deserve this? Nothin'! Stuck here for three years when I was just trying to get home. *Still* just wanna get home, take care of my mama.

RUBY: I wanna see my family, too, so stop takin' your anger out on us.

JIMMY: You the only ones here.

RUBY: Why can't you just be nice like you were when we were datin'?

JIMMY: I can't just sit around rockin' some dead doll and diggin' into some abyss of useless boxes. I need to move. To pulse. To fight if I have to just to be aware.

RUBY: I don't want to be aware.

JIMMY: Now you're just lyin'. Everybody wants to be aware. Otherwise you just be dead.

RUBY: Yeah?

JIMMY: Yeah!

RUBY: The three of us are stuck here, surrounded by blackness when we should be surrounded by light. We should be goin' home, with our families. Don't even know *why* we're here and it hurts.

PRENTISS: Being aware is about connection. Sometimes it's worth the hurt.

JIMMY: Maybe that's why Blue always lookin' in those boxes. Be aware of somethin'.

PRENTISS: I'm aware that you were just another Dooney Boy, D.

JIMMY: You don't know a damn thing about me so watch what you're sayin'.

PRENTISS rises, stands toe-to-toe with JIMMY.

PRENTISS: What are you gonna do? Beat me up? Kill me, D?

JIMMY: Kill you? I ain't never killed nobody. You're Blue. How many kills you got?

PRENTISS abruptly turns away.

JIMMY: Oh, see, now he don't wanna be talkin' to me cuz I hit a raw spot, huh, Blue? That why you always in them boxes, searchin' for your kills?

RUBY: Stop arguing. For God's sake. Isn't it bad enough that another hurricane is on the way. We need to get out of here. We need to go home!

Stage lights lower as single down-light comes up center stage. RUBY walks into light, sits with doll. A loud helicopter and sloshing water are heard in flashback.

RUBY: No, ma, stop yellin'! I ain't that stupid. Leastwise not about goin' back into the attic.

She rocks doll as a child's haunting sing-song voice is heard.

CHILD'S VOICE: (off-stage sing-song haunting nursery rhyme voice) Mother, may I go out to swim?

RUBY: We gonna be okay, baby. We got to be. I gotta talk to Jimmy.

CHILD'S VOICE: (off-stage sing-song haunting nursery rhyme voice) Yes, my darling daughter.

RUBY: I need my phone. Maybe Jimmy and me can figure this all out then be together again…even if home is this damn roof. Stupid Katrina flooding everything.

CHILD'S VOICE: (off-stage sing-song haunting nursery rhyme voice) Fold your clothes up neat and trim…

RUBY: Wonder if I can swim in the window and get my phone.

RUBY rises, leaves doll on floor, and steps to edge of the light.

RUBY: Water's not that high. (beat) What ma? No! I didn't say nothin'.

CHILD'S VOICE: (off-stage sing-song nursery rhyme voice)…but don't go near the water.

Down-light cuts out. A single splash is heard. The helicopter and water sounds fade. RUBY crosses back to box, hugs doll. Stage lights up as flashback ends.

JIMMY: We all wanna go home, girl. Been wantin' that for three years since Katrina. Get home to mama.

PRENTISS: You think you deserve to go home, D?

JIMMY: I said watch what you're sayin', Blue.

JIMMY crosses quickly to PRENTISS who rises. They stand toe-to-toe.

PRENTISS: Get out of my face or I'll - -

JIMMY: You'll what? Throw fire and brimstone at me now cuz I'm all in your shit? Stop searchin' those papers for some story or file? Or *explanation?* Or *ghost?* What, Blue? What?

PRENTISS: I don't have to tell you what I'm looking for, D. You think I don't know who you are? I know that before Katrina you and your krewe were tearing up New Orleans in a war with 3 'n' G. You know how many people were killed because of you? You know how many cops? Do you?

JIMMY: Is that what you're tryin' to find in those papers? If I killed anyone? Why you doin' that?

PRENTISS: Never mind what I'm doing. You don't know me.

JIMMY: If you think you know me then I think I can know you. You probably one those cops whose always on the take. You skim a little here, slide a little there. Same everlastin' bullshit happenin' in N.O.P.D. for years. And you right there blazin' in the middle. Takin', skimmin', slidin', killin' - -

PRENTISS: I never killed anyone until...

JIMMY: Till what? Blue?

RUBY: Stop it, Jimmy, for God' sake.

JIMMY: God got nothin' to do with this! Think you're gonna find God in that box? Lemme see if I find him in a box.

JIMMY pushes PRENTISS, crosses to the 2008 box, pulls out newspapers, reads random articles.

JIMMY: Let's see...January "Wandering Toddler's Mother Arrested"...No God there. Seems some people don't wanna take care of their kids - -

RUBY: You don't know that. Some people can only do - -

JIMMY ignores RUBY, grabs and throws papers from box.

JIMMY: March..."LSU Kicks Off Spring Practice." Okay, maybe there's hope for God there.

JIMMY grabs and throws more papers.

We got a garage fire, rape suspect, bad education system, yeah, no surprise there, and no God. June..."Displaced Residents Hold Listening Session." I bet they trying to get God to listen cuz you know government don't. "Thief Drives Stolen Squad Car into River"

JIMMY laughs sarcastically

Oh, Blue, there's got to be God there. But no God last month at a murder in Tremé...

JIMMY suddenly stops. PAUSE.

No. God.

RUBY: We have to have hope.

JIMMY: (confused) What?

RUBY: Hope to get home. Be with family.

JIMMY, visibly upset, looks from newspaper to RUBY and back again.

RUBY: I might see my ma.

PRENTISS: I had Buddy B., my dog. Just the two of us. Hope he made it.

RUBY: You might see your ma, Jimmy. *Hope.*

RUBY grabs JIMMY'S arm. He pushes her away, trembles.

JIMMY: Maybe you all can have hope.

RUBY: You can, too.

JIMMY: No.

RUBY: Yes.

JIMMY: *No.* Maybe you still got peoples out there who can pull you out of this nightmare. Wanna know what I think? I think we been forgotten.

RUBY: I won't believe that. You have to have hope that we can get out of here, get home, be with family.

JIMMY: Ain't gonna see mama.

RUBY: You don't know that.

JIMMY: Ain't gonna see mama.

RUBY: Hope is the only chance we get!

JIMMY: *Ain't seein' her!* Know why? Cuz she's up at Holt, in the ground. Pauper's cemetery. Wanna know how I know?

Waves the newspaper

Because it's in this damned paper! I told you nothin' good be comin' outta them boxes you readin'.

Opens newspaper and reads.

"A Tremé woman died from a single gunshot through the front door of a home. The victim, identified as…Jamesa Bisette was…shot shortly after midnight in the 1100 block of North Roman Street in Tremé." (beat) You wanna hear more? No, I didn't think so. She's dead and you don't know a damn thing about me and my family, girl. Neither of you do!

JIMMY chokes up.

I ain't gonna see her. I ain't.

RUBY: I'm sorry. I didn't know.

JIMMY: (wipes his eyes, trying to recover) Damn right.

RUBY: But I can't believe we been forgotten. It's human nature to hope.

JIMMY: You think we still human? We're dead! D-E-A-D! Dead! You drowned probably so bloated nobody can identify what's left. I was out with no I.D. or nothin' on me cuz how's I supposed to know I ain't gonna make it back home. And Blue's dog ain't gonna show up barking for him and his exploded heart! And tryin' to act all normal, reading newspapers, playing with that damn doll, holdin' on to the hope of God helpin' get us home ain't gonna change that. I lost my life. I lost my mama. Hope gone, girl.

RUBY: But we're in this together. Connected.

PRENTISS: Aware.

RUBY: Maybe...maybe...

JIMMY: Maybe what? You gonna go all princess on me, again? Say something all nice like you know somethin'. The hell with you.

RUBY: (struggling to make sense) Maybe I don't know nothin' accept that we *are* in this together. I don't know why but maybe...maybe we have to just accept that whatever happens - -

JIMMY: How you be acceptin' death? Tell me, Ruby. How?

RUBY: (near tears) I don't know but I'm scared that if we don't, then you're right, evil wins and we'll never find our way home.

JIMMY: Evil already won. Got no more family. Mama's dead.

PRENTISS: Death is the only guarantee in life.

JIMMY: What you say, Blue?

PRENTISS: Nothing.

JIMMY: You do and say an awful lot of nothin'. Make me wonder what you hidin'.

RUBY: Don't start again, you two. Please.

101

JIMMY crosses to turn on the radio.

RADIO ANNOUNCER: Despite a declared emergency, some New Orleanians won't give up the music. *The Forgivin' Blues Band* will play tonight in a free concert at Lafayette Square featuring their remake of the old spiritual "The Truth Shall Set You Free." As Hurricane Gustav rages, we all need some *Forgivin'*.

The first, gospel-revival strings of "The Truth Shall Set You Free" are heard from radio. All listen as JIMMY softly runs one hand along the radio and wipes eyes with other hand.

> The truth shall set you free
> Then you will know the truth,
> and the truth will set you free.
> Then you will know the truth,
> and the truth will set you free.

JIMMY: My mama loves…loved…*Forgivin' Blues*.

JIMMY lowers volume then shuts off radio. Suddenly, PRENTISS rises, holding a newspaper in his hands. He reads intensely on an inner page. He is noticeably disturbed by what he has read.

RUBY: Mr. Prentiss, you okay?

JIMMY: Maybe he find his own hell and damnation in that abyss. (beat) Blue?

PRENTISS: Leave me alone!

JIMMY rushes PRENTISS. They grapple. JIMMY rips newspaper out of PRENTISS' hands. He scans it.

JIMMY: This is an article about me. About those cops. They buried it way back here in the paper. (beat) You had to be searchin' for this for three years. Why?

PRENTISS: It wasn't supposed to happen this way.

JIMMY: These cops got off a killin' me and you all interested. What do you know, Blue?

PRENTISS: Jimmy.

JIMMY: What you callin' me Jimmy for? You ain't never called me Jimmy.

PRENTISS: I'm sorry.

JIMMY drops newspaper, grabs PRENTISS, spins him to face him.

PRENTISS: I wasn't sure. I had to be sure.

Stage lights lower as two single down-lights come up, each at downstage right and left – one holds a window frame and case of water. The other holds a handgun and police officer's badge and/or cap. JIMMY and PRENTISS split, each walking into one light of the flashback. The sounds of chaos – yelling, helicopter, sloshing waters – are heard in the background. PRENTISS puts on hat/badge and picks up handgun. JIMMY steps through the window.

JIMMY: Got to be water in here.

PRENTISS: (speaks with determination) I do solemnly declare that I will act at all times to the best manner befitting a police officer.

JIMMY searches, picks up water.

JIMMY: Hell of a heavy case. Now maybe somethin' to eat.

PRENTISS: (speaks with determination) I will preserve the dignity and will respect the rights of all individuals.

JIMMY searches, hugging water.

JIMMY: Mama likes her Zapp's Cajun Dill chips.

PRENTISS: (speaks with determination) I will discharge my duties with integrity and will promote understanding and goodwill.

Loud gunfire heard. JIMMY ducks.

JIMMY: What the hell you shooting at us for?

PRENTISS: (voice shakes slightly) I will exercise my authority as a police officer in the manner intended by law.

Loud, yet different, gunfire is heard. PRENTISS grabs his chest, his knees wobble.

JIMMY: Hey, don't be shootin' back, fools. Where's the back door?

PRENTISS: (voice is shakier) I will faithfully obey the orders of my superiors and will confront danger in the line of duty.

PRENTISS' breathing gets labored. He moves hand from chest and painfully draws a gun, gets in firing stance.

JIMMY: Hell! I just want to get some water and food to my mama. Make sure she okay, that she not flooded out.

JIMMY breaks through window still holding water. He spins around, trying to find his bearings, stops facing downstage.

PRENTISS: (voice is shakes with stilted breath) I will act justly and impartially. I will constantly strive to honor this oath and be aware in my service as a police officer.

PRENTISS fires a single shot. The sound is deafening, gunfire and exploding water bottles. JIMMY, shocked, opens his hands dropping the water and grabs his stomach as PRENTISS, grasping at his heart, slips to the ground. JIMMY slips to ground. The actor's area lights fade as flashback ends. PRENTISS removes badge/hat, sets down handgun. JIMMY and PRENTISS rise, cross back to their positions before the flashback. Stage lights up. JIMMY has just spun PRENTISS, they are facing each other. RUBY picks up the newspaper article, reads.

RUBY: "Katrina struck on Aug. 29, 2005. In its aftermath, chaos gripped the city and looting was reported as citizens struggled to get food and water. Police Officers acknowledged shooting at people, but said they did so only after taking fire they thought was directed at them. With conflicting testimony of events and little evidence, the case of Jimmy Bisette was dismissed. It is the latest in a series of emotional criminal prosecutions tied to Katrina that have fizzled."

JIMMY: Fizzled? Fizzled? I died!

RUBY: Oh my God.

PRENTISS: So did I.

JIMMY: You deserved it!

PRENTISS: And you didn't.

JIMMY: I know that!

PRENTISS: And I know that, too. *Now.* That article. It says you never had a record. Never.

JIMMY: I told you that, Blue! I never killed no one! I told you!

PRENTISS: I was trying to justify it. If I found something that said...I didn't know. I was just doing my job. It was all I had. No friends. No family. Just my job. My dog. (beat) Everything was crazy. Everyone was crazy. I had orders. Orders. I didn't know. Jimmy. I didn't know I killed you.

JIMMY: I'm gonna kill *you.*

JIMMY hits PRENTISS hard. PRENTISS falls. JIMMY jumps on top, beating PRENTISS' chest/heart. RUBY pulls at JIMMY.

RUBY: Jimmy, stop it! *Stop!* He's already dead. *We're already dead!* Jimmy!

JIMMY and PRENTISS roll into the table, knocking the radio off. The radio crackles to life.

RADIO ANNOUNCER: As the city of New Orleans continues its Post-K afterlife, victims of Katrina will finally be laid to rest in the new mausoleums and memorial built to honor Katrina victims.

JIMMY stops choking PRENTISS but still holds fast. RUBY holds fast to JIMMY. THEY all look at radio.

RADIO ANNOUNCER: (continues) The 85 bodies that went unclaimed sat in caskets in a refrigerated warehouse the past three years.

RUBY sinks to the ground. JIMMY rolls off of PRENTISS. PRENTISS sits up, rubbing his throat.

RADIO ANNOUNCER: (continues) Yesterday, the majority of the bodies were taken by hearse to the mausoleums. As another August ends, today the final three will laid to rest in a New Orleans jazz funeral. At last, these souls will find their ways home. (beat) In other news, Hurricane Gustav has decreased to a Category 2 and its track is uncertain, so officials are not ready to make evacuation decisions just yet.

JIMMY rises, shuts radio off.

RUBY: Us. He means us.

PRENTISS: Jimmy, if I had a chance, I'd take it all back.

JIMMY: This is the only chance we get. To be aware. You're right, Ruby. It hurts.

PRENTISS: I'm sorry.

JIMMY: Doesn't quite make up for it. Does it, Blue? You're going to have to answer up above.

PRENTISS: Can you forgive me? Here and now? I searched three years hoping the truth would set me free of this guilt. Instead...Jimmy...I hope you can...

RUBY: Forgive.

JIMMY: (with softness) Goin' princess again?

JIMMY helps RUBY to her feet.

RUBY nods. JIMMY slowly nods.

RUBY: Jimmy. The radio said new mausoleums.

JIMMY: What?

RUBY: Not in the ground like Holt. This is our way out. No more flooding over us. We'll be raised up. Home.

JIMMY: Maybe I'll see my mama.

RUBY: Maybe I'll see my baby.

JIMMY: Baby?

RUBY: Our baby. If I hadn't died.

JIMMY: But we broke up Memorial Day. Three months before the storm.

RUBY: Remember Stallings Playground? Last day of Jazz Fest? I was four months along when I died.

JIMMY: I would have been a papa? A papa. (beat) That's why you won't let go of that doll.

RUBY nods. JIMMY holds her tenderly.

JIMMY: We'll see our baby. Family.

RUBY hugs tight to JIMMY and doll.

RUBY: Baby. Family. My God. I think we're goin' home.

The gospel-revival "The Truth Shall Set You Free" plays as the light fade:

> The truth shall set you free
> Then you will know the truth,
> and the truth will set you free.
> Then you will know the truth,
> and the truth will set you free.

Lights fade.

END OF PLAY

SWORD PLAY

Inspired by Charles Hartley - Nürnberg Cathedral

CAST OF CHARACTERS

MAEVE: 23 years old. Irish-American, no accent. Dressed in white blouse covered by a simple, bibbed, long black dress with a wimple on her head. In her first postulancy, perhaps on her way to becoming a nun but not yet fully committed to the vocation. Hopeful of the good in the world.

AARON: 7 years old. African-American. Dressed in simple, hand-me-down play-clothes of the era. Boisterous and not afraid to say what he thinks.

FATHER DOLAN: 68 years old. Old-school, Irish-born Catholic priest. Dressed in severe black priest's clothing. He recently re-located from Virginia to New Orleans but longs for his home in Boston.

TIME

Hot August afternoon. 1962.

SETTING

The sanctuary of a Catholic Church, New Orleans, LA. A simple set of wooden benches can represent pews.

───────────────

In darkness the sound of a laughing child is heard, mingled with what sounds like a mother's laughter and a clashing of wood on wood. Lights wash on stage as a storm would brew: rising from black to purple to gray-blue. MAEVE, carrying a wooden sword, runs through the pews playing tag with AARON who also carries a wooden sword.

AARON: You'll never catch me.

MAEVE: I will. I will.

AARON: You're too slow sister.

MAEVE: I'm *not* a sister *yet* but I *am* fleet of foot to do God's work.

AARON: Ha. You're funny! Catch me if you can!

> *AARON is quick but MAEVE sneaks a double-back, catching him.*

MAEVE: Who's funny now?

AARON: (laughing) You ain't even.

> *MAEVE "noogies" AARON, he giggles. FATHER DOLAN enter with a box of bibles. AARON spins from MAEVE, raises his sword.*

AARON: I'm a pirate. On the guard.

MAEVE: (silly-fake French accent) You mean en garde. A French expression.

AARON: We ain't even French. We're Irish.

MAEVE: Yes. We are. You'll always be my little Irish boy.

FATHER DOLAN: Sister Maeve.

AARON turns sword at FATHER DOLAN who raises the box as if to defend himself.

FATHER DOLAN: (playfully) Young pirate, do not point that sword at me.

MAEVE puts her sword on a pew. PAUSE then AARON bursts into laughter.

AARON: Geez, Father, you look like you seen a ghost.

FATHER DOLAN puts the bibles down.

FATHER DOLAN: Only the holy ghost, my son.

AARON: Anyways, we were just funning.

FATHER DOLAN: I have fond memories of playing treasure hunt in the seminary sanctuary at St. John's in Boston.

AARON: So you're kinda a pirate, too.

FATHER DOLAN chuckles.

MAEVE: Actually we're celebrating. Father.

FATHER DOLAN: Celebrating?

MAEVE: Yes. Two years after New Orleans public schools but the archdiocese has made a good decision. And you've joined us right at this turning point. How's your first week with us, Father? I'll bet New Orleans is a bit of a shock...I mean is it different from Virginia?

FATHER DOLAN: Different. Yes. And a bit of a shock might be a good turn of a phrase. I had expected transfer to Boston but Bishops sometimes have funny senses of humor.

AARON: I like funny people.

FATHER DOLAN: Silly pirates, perhaps. But not Bishops who trade priests with no thought to my desires for home. First Virginia. Now New Orleans. They never send me to Boston. But I'll make St. Mary's a sanctuary for our people and then, perhaps...(beat) Please ignore this old pirate going on. What are we celebrating?

AARON: Being Irish.

FATHER DOLAN: You are not Irish, my son.

AARON: I live here with a Irish nun and a wrinkled old...um, I mean a Irish priest. Don't that make me Irish? Ain't there negro Irish in the world?

MAEVE: Of course there are.

AARON: Let's go play swords in the choir loft.

FATHER DOLAN: I am not sure that is a wise choice.

MAEVE: We can take the sword play to the playground, yes?

AARON: But the choir loft is the mast of me *piiii-rate* ship.

AARON dashes off-stage.

MAEVE: (calling out) Be careful. Please.

FATHER DOLAN unpacks box, handing bibles to MAEVE who distributes them on the pews, on and off, throughout play.

FATHER DOLAN: You did not answer my question. Celebrating?

MAEVE: The decision by Archbishop Rummel. Aaron will get to go to school right here at St. Mary's. Desegregation. The power of prayer, Father.

FATHER DOLAN: I am not sure desegregation is the Lord's way.

AARON runs on stage with the sword, he trips, falls, and laughs boisterously.

AARON: Catch me if you can!

AARON dashes off stage.

FATHER DOLAN: Exactly why *this must* happen.

MAEVE hugs a bible.

MAEVE: I agree Father. Of course. Two years since the public schools joined across race lines and, now, blessedly

Aaron will have a fuller life than I had growing up here //

FATHER DOLAN: Sister //

MAEVE: Not that my life was...I mean...I've loved my life here but now he'll go to school right where he's grown these months.

FATHER DOLAN: Sister //

MAEVE: We'll read together. I'll help with his homework. Guide his spiritual life. Make his projects together - -

FATHER DOLAN: (with insistence) Sister!

MAEVE: (takes a subservient stance) I'm so sorry Father.

FATHER DOLAN: Your enthusiasm for the young pirate and his well being are commendable and will bear worthy for our next move.

MAEVE: Our next move?

FATHER DOLAN: St. Augustine Church is sending someone over this morning.

MAEVE: For?

THEY distribute bibles from box.

FATHER DOLAN: Tell me, how is your formation process coming along?

MAEVE: My formation?

FATHER DOLAN: If I am to create a sanctuary for our people then I should know more about you and the others who serve this parish. Don't you agree?

MAEVE: Yes, Father. But forgive. I thought we were talking about Aaron. What does St. Augustine have to do with - -

FATHER DOLAN: (with insistence) Formation. Now.

MAEVE: I'm ending the first year of my Postulancy.

FATHER DOLAN: Good. So on to your Novitiate.

MAEVE: Well. Not. No. I mean. Mother Superior feels I need another Postulancy year for transition. To truly feel the love and spirit of our Lord.

FATHER DOLAN: I see. And where do you see your future, beyond sword play in the sanctuary?

MAEVE: Mother Superior says I like being in the community much more than my reflections and prayers. I've been guiding the children's spiritual life in Sunday school. I'm captain of the parish volleyball team which can be challenging in my habit. Its been wonderful having Aaron in my life. Just getting out with him and other families. I know it's a sadness that his mother abandoned him on our doorstep but he brings me such joy. His laughter fills the empty spaces.

AARON crosses, sword slashing the air.

AARON: Hey, sister, c'mon.

FATHER DOLAN: She'll be along when we are finished.

AARON: Let's do pirate hide and seek. You hide first.

AARON runs off-stage. Muffled counting is heard.

FATHER DOLAN: What do you mean by empty spaces?

MAEVE: Perhaps I should go play with - -

FATHER DOLAN holds up his hand, shakes his head 'no'. MAEVE hugs bible.

MAEVE: I'm sorry I said anything, Father. I'm being silly. I love my life here. I do. (pause as she hugs a bible) It's just...the days are long. Longer than I thought they'd be. I expected more sureness on my path towards devotion.

FATHER DOLAN: Yes. As I thought. You are early in your formation. Have not yet made your full commitment to our Lord.

MAEVE: I don't mean to have doubts. These questions between what I thought this life would be and what it is.

FATHER DOLAN: A life of servitude must have sacrifice.

MAEVE: Yes, Father. And New Orleans instead of Boston?

FATHER DOLAN: (nodding) Sacrifice. Which brings me to the young pirate.

MAEVE: At first Mother Superior wanted to put him in the dormitory but we had no other children there six months ago. I offered the extra cot in my cell. It's a miracle how he's blossomed. He loves to read. We plant in the garden. Visit the neighborhoods. Have you been to Tremé, yet, Father? An amazing community full of history and architecture. I'm taking him to Myrtle Street Playground to see what other mothers are doing. I can't believe our good blessings - -

FATHER DOLAN: You came to this place as a child yourself. Also...left on the convent steps.

MAEVE: Raised and educated by the sisters. It seems natural for me to follow their path. I stayed mainly cloistered up until last year when I went to Albany.

FATHER DOLAN: Albany?

MAEVE: Georgia. With Southern Christian Leadership. Protest against segregation.

FATHER DOLAN: Oh dear. I fear you *are* confused and now you have grown all too fond of the boy.

MAEVE: Aaron brings me...we bring each other a sense of...belonging.

AARON'S counting stops.

AARON: (off-stage voice) Ready or not. Here I come.

FATHER DOLAN: Perhaps you tend to him with a zeal that speaks to your own desire for something outside the church.

MAEVE: He needs a mother - -

FATHER DOLAN: Mother?

MAEVE: Figure. A mother *figure.*

FATHER DOLAN: But he is different.

AARON runs on stage with sword.

AARON: You ain't even found no good hiding place! I can see you right here! My turn. Come find me.

AARON dashes off stage. MAEVE smiles towards AARON, anxious to join him. FATHER DOLAN stops her with his gaze.

FATHER DOLAN: You are young. I can see how you might confuse your commitment to our Lord with your commitment to the boy. But you cannot allow one soul to override the good we must do for all souls. Our Father will fill your emptiness once the boy leaves.

MAEVE: Leaves?

FATHER DOLAN: St. Augustine will be sending someone for him.

MAEVE: For him? Father. You're not taking him...away from me?

FATHER DOLAN: It is not away from you. It is towards what is best for him. To a family with St. Augustine. A family...like the boy.

MAEVE: But he has a chance for a life here.

FATHER DOLAN: And what would that life be?

MAEVE: Growing up with love and devotion beyond measure. Having a spiritual life which is also fun. Connecting with other children to learn. (beat) Being with me.

FATHER DOLAN: Was your life growing in this orphanage as ideal as you describe it?

PAUSE as MAEVE considers this. SHE has the slightest shake of her head 'no'.

FATHER DOLAN: The family from St. Augustine are *his* people. They will give the boy more than we can within the confines of these walls. They will understand him. What society holds for him. Allows him. *Dictates* of him. He will be with his own people. I know this is difficult for you to understand but all things are not black and white.

MAEVE: You're talking as if they are.

FATHER DOLAN: You cannot care for him as his own kind can. You cannot hope to teach him what society demands of him. And making an example of him attending St. Mary's next month - -

MAEVE: An example? Father, I'm not. He'll get the best education here - -

FATHER DOLAN: Among students and teachers who don't want him. Don't you see?

MAEVE: We're all the same in the eyes of God.

FATHER DOLAN: We're talking of society.

MAEVE: God and society should be one.

FATHER DOLAN: You will not preach to me.

MAEVE: I didn't mean - -

FATHER DOLAN: Do you not think I have considered the best interests of boy in this decision?

MAEVE slams down a bible.

MAEVE: No. I don't. I know what's best for him!

FATHER DOLAN: I will allow your outburst because you are upset, Maeve, but you will remember your place in our Father's House. And in my parish. Do you understand?

MAEVE: No. I don't understand. You just got here. You can't go changing everything. For over one hundred years The Sisters of St. Mary have been serving this parish, caring for community, even taking in and raising abandoned children. I don't see how you can send Aaron to others just because of the color of his skin. This is 1962. We're integrating the schools. Aaron will have friends of all colors.

FATHER DOLAN: You are being naive.

MAEVE: Just because you believe in some archaic sense of separation doesn't mean I'm being naive.

FATHER DOLAN: Were you here when the public schools integrated?

MAEVE: (nods) I stood toe-to-toe with the protestors and I'd do it again.

FATHER DOLAN: Precisely my point, Maeve.

MAEVE: *Sister* Maeve.

FATHER DOLAN: Perhaps. (beat) If you do not think we will see the same reactions next month then you are, indeed, being naive.

MAEVE: What do you know about it? You're not even from here.

FATHER DOLAN: New Orleans is not the only place with race issues. Prior to coming here I was priest at Sacred Heart Church in Meherrin, Virginia. I was under consideration for a Boston appointment. Then, officials of Prince Edward

County closed the public schools rather than integrate them and parishioners chose sides. Chose battles. Battles in my parish. I saw many people hurt: physically, emotionally, and most especially spiritually and I will not allow that to happen here. (beat) You think me harsh but I am educated to the circumstances. I have a chance to create a safe haven for our people.

MAEVE: *Our* people? Stop saying that!

FATHER DOLAN: It is best. And *you*. Are *not*. His *mother*.

MAEVE: What?

FATHER DOLAN: You will *not* be going to Myrtle Street Playground to see, as you put it, what other mothers are doing.

MAEVE: I didn't mean…for Christ's sake.

FATHER DOLAN: Maeve! (beat) I see the influences of the society around us changing the servitude of our sisters, our parishioners.

MAEVE: Of course society should change us. We can't live in the past anymore, cloistered off from the world. We're part of the world.

FATHER DOLAN: Is that what you think your life in service to our Lord will be? Caring for *those* people?

MAEVE: I always thought my life would be God *and* people. Together. Genesis says "If as one people speaking the same language they have begun to do this, then nothing they plan to do will be impossible for them."

FATHER DOLAN: "I will make a distinction between my people and your people." Exodus. And if you feel as though you need to help those people, perhaps you would be best taking some time away from the church to figure your place. Choose your sacrifice.

MAEVE: "To do what is right and just is more acceptable to the Lord than sacrifice." Proverbs.

FATHER DOLAN: Enough! How dare you quote scriptures to me! You will lose that sanctimonious tone or I will see to it that your first Postulancy is your last. This house will not be another Meherrin falling apart as race lines are drawn. This will be a place of sanctuary and when the Bishop sees so, I'll get to go home!

AARON bursts in, sword slashing.

AARON: You never found me. I win! Take that!

FATHER DOLAN: (to MAEVE) You have no choice. (beat) Young pirate. Come here.

AARON stops slashing.

AARON: Whatcha want, Father Pirate?

MAEVE steps between them.

FATHER DOLAN: If you feel you must, I will allow you to tell him. Then be in my office in one hour and we will discuss your future in this parish. You will learn sacrifice.

FATHER DOLAN exits with authority, taking the empty box with him. MAEVE deflates. PAUSE.

AARON: What's he meanin', sister?

MAEVE: Aaron.

AARON: You ain't lookin' so happy.

MAEVE: I'm always happy when you're around. My...my son.

AARON: Ha! You're funny. You ain't even Negro.

MAEVE: I ain't even.

AARON picks up MAEVE'S sword from pew.

AARON: We can play pirates in the choir loft.

MAEVE: Aaron - -

MAEVE touches his arm. PAUSE.

AARON: Why you look like you seen a ghost?

MAEVE: Aaron. Father Dolan has made a decision about…about you. You and your life. Your life here at the convent.

AARON: I like livin' with you. I'd live with you anywheres. (beat) I don't wanna go to people at St. Augustine.

MAEVE: You were listening?

AARON nods, point up to the choir loft.

MAEVE: Hard not to hear the echoes from the choir loft. One of your favorite spots.

AARON: We can go live in Tremé right by the playground.

MAEVE: But what if Father Dolan is right? Maybe the people from St. Augustine can teach you more than I can. And I should spend more time with the Lord.

AARON: You ain't even gonna be no sister, anyways. You're too fun. Not all wrinkled up like the other sisters and that old father. You ain't chicken neither, Sister. You're one of the best fighters I know but you don't fool me. You'd never hurt a fly and nobody gonna teach me more than you. Can we play pirates, now? Me and you, sister?

MAEVE: I ain't even. (beat) Aaron, we're going to Myrtle Street playground but, first, we should go pack some bags.

AARON: Where we goin'?

MAEVE: On a pirate adventure.

AARON hands MAEVE her swords, grabs his sword. They cross blades and smile.

Lights fade.

END OF PLAY

JINGLE OF A MOMENT

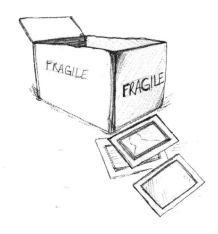

CHARACTER

HANNAH: 35 to 55 years old. Dressed in jeans and a SNOW WHITE T-shirt.

TIME

Present day. An economically depressed city or town near city/town of performance.

SETTING

A stack of newspapers on a black stage. One cardboard box with large "Fragile" written on side in black marker is hidden behind her chair. Several photographs in varying, expensive frames. One chair. HANNAH has a cell phone.

PRODUCTION NOTE

As HANNAH looks at photographs in her hands, if possible the images should project behind her for audience to see. If not possible, HANNAH refers to photo. Photos are:

1. HANNAH and SHAUN laughing, young
2. Nieces and Nephews
3. SHAUN wearing tool belt at work
4. HANNAH small and sick, treatments for cancer
5. 1951 F1 Pickup truck
6. HANNAH and SHAUN not happy - grey haze
7. Same as previous photo however SHAUN fades or cuts out and HANNAH is left alone

---

Lights sprinkle up in a haze of blue and grey coolness. HANNAH is surrounded by newspaper stacks and photo frames as, throughout the monologue, she reflects on photos.

HANNAH speaks to audience.

HANNAH: (to phone) Ring. Ring. Ring!

Our whole lives can change in the jingle of a moment. You know what I mean. The phone call that says your loved one is safe from harm. The doctor calls with news about those tests. My husband calling to say we got the job...or not. *That's* the one phone call that can change our whole lives.

HANNAH picks up photograph 1 of SHAUN and her in the first few months of their relationship, reflects on it.

Our whole lives. Shaun. My husband.

Wow. We are so young in this picture. Sixteen. High school sweethearts.

I always believed we'd have a fairy tale life. Together. Happily ever after. Prince Charming rides up on his white stead, saves Snow White, then all their memories are beautiful.

Those *memories* are what should matter. Not these expensive frames that are not just...things.

If projected, image fades. HANNAH looks at phone.

Ring!

Then there's Rapunzel. Imprisoned by a witch in a tower. "Rapunzel, Rapunzel, let down your hair." That long, lavish hair. Maybe if she was more positive things would have been different.

What do you think? Being positive can change things, can't it?

Although...I'm not sure if positive thinking is going to help Shaun and me to continue to be...

Prince Charming and Snow White.

Points to phone.

The last fairy-size glimmer of positive thinking.

I *can't* give up. I'm a *happy* person, dammit.

BEAT

See, I have this bold, uninhibited laugh. I never really thought much about it. It's just my laugh. I don't cultivate it or fake it or make it grow by doing some weird diaphragm movements.

HANNAH pushes on diaphragm, making funny breath sounds.

But with a laugh like that, you have to be positive, right? My laugh. Wanna hear it?

HANNAH laughs long and heartily.

I've had comedians ask if I could tour with them as their laugh person. Ha! Should have taken them up on that. Steady income from laughing. Can you imagine that?

Looks at, shakes phone. Sighs. Picks up photograph 2 with nieces and nephews, laughs, reflects on photo.

Oh, my laugh can be a bit of embarrassment to some people. Our nieces and nephews don't sit with me at funny movies.

For awhile, I stifled my laugh. Believing people who were embarrassed. I tried giggles instead of guffaws. It didn't last. Couldn't really. You know what I mean, don't you?

If projected, image fades.

You shouldn't change because someone makes you *feel* like you have to. You should only change for you.

The problem, though, is sometimes outside forces can *make* you change.

BEAT

No. No. I refuse to let that happen.

I'm going to be positive and so are you. I need you to. I mean, we're all in this together. Right? Neighbor to neighbor. If we're positive maybe good things *can* happen.

HANNAH picks up photograph 3 of SHAUN with tool belt on, working at a job-site, reflects on photo.

Why does a man always looks hot in a tool-belt?

A construction wizard, my Shaun. It's his art, really. Strong, solid foundations that hold up people's hearts in their castles. Being able to do that is part of who he is.

Shaun is always the optimist.

BEAT

Was.

Was. Always the optimist.

Believing in people. Seeing the good in them.

I love him for that.

The *worst* from the past six years is it took my warm, generous husband and changed him.

Somewhere along the way, he lost the capacity to dream.

I wonder what dreams cost. Can any of us afford them these days?

If projected, image fades.

CHANTING

Ring, ring, ring, ring, ring, ring, ring.

Somewhere in my crazy, I think if *you* do the positive thinking *with* me then we'll be in this together and things *will change*.

I read about this research study a few years back that found success is like 90 percent attitude. The *collective* positive thinking, *more* than one person, neighbors coming together will make a difference. We can do that. Can't we?

HANNAH looks at photograph on top of pile but shies away from it.

Its not like this is some dreaded disease.

Or. Is it?

BEAT

I *have* been there. Done that.

I forgot Shaun took that photo. He said I looked…peaceful. All wrapped up, trying to keep warm. And then he put his arms around me.

Forces herself to pick up photograph 4 of herself, wrapped in blankets, sipping tea, trying to keep safe. She gently reflects on photo.

We waited on a lot of phone calls back then, too.

Survived.

And came out with a positive attitude. This is going to sound crazy to people who've never had cancer but I'm thankful to have gone through that. It made me who I am.

Who I still want to be.

A fighter. An adventurer. An optimist. A believer in humanity and spirit. Easy to laughter. A positive thinker.

Oh, don't get me wrong, there were days when I screamed at the randomness of it. Days when Shaun and I melted into each other's arms fighting the weakness and poison and confusion. But when you have cancer you have to fight. Shaun and me against the world.

There is one thing we couldn't fight. We have nieces and nephews. Not *our* children. Chemo. Radiation.

If projected, image fades.

I am not crazy.

I…*we*…survived cancer. We accepted never having children. We loved each other more.

So we can survive anything. Right?

PASUE

But cancer was one year out of our lives.

Not six years of being beaten down. Six years of no work. No money. No peace. Six years of "pull yourself up by the bootstraps."

I am pulling and pulling and pulling. I am. For both of us.

It brought us together for awhile. In the beginning. We clung to each other in the dark forest. Telling each other it was going to be okay.

But a body, a mind, a soul can only take so much. I want to stop being scared we'll lose our home. That Shaun will lose his hard-working Irish foundation. I'll lose my sanity. Stop being scared that we'll never recover and everything we've worked decades to build *together* will disappear in the evil witch's cauldron.

I don't want to have to box up our life to sell to the highest bidder in the hope that we can stop the bank from foreclosing.

I don't want to lose my husband because the only things we ever seem to talk about anymore are the problems. After six years they're pulling us apart. What relationship can survive this?

BEAT

What if I'm Rapunzel, stuck in the tower, and now I'm bald?

No escape except maybe...one phone call.

PASUE

To many people, to a lot of you, what we're going through is an...

Abstraction.

Something you hear about but don't feel. You can turn the channel. Open a new web-page. Toss the newspaper. Close the front door.

Abstraction.

It was to me.

HANNAH points at photograph on pile.

This. This. Is when it changed. When I saw the change in him.

HANNAH picks up photograph 5 of truck, reflects on photo.

Shaun's 50th birthday and I found a glimmer of hope. The perfect coach for my prince: a 1951 Ford truck.

He'd always wanted one, that connection to history, and built-Ford-tough. Throwing his fishing pole in the back heading to the river. Long country drives together. And, as if by a sprinkling of fairy dust, that truck appeared. Meadow Green. Original engine. And not a lot of money for what it was. I got the financing on a wing and a prayer. When his birthday dawned, and the surprise was sprung, the excitement I had hoped for…

…simply wasn't there.

Why? He asked the cost.

That's when I knew my prince charming had been changed.

The coach for my prince? For sale. Hoping someone buys it before the repo guy shows up.

Happy Birthday.

If projected, image fades.

HANNAH picks up photograph 6 of SHAUN and her in a grey haze, not working, not happy.

I miss the laughter in his eyes.

HANNAH sadly hugs the photo to her.

It isn't supposed to be this way.

We did everything right.

Dared to dream. Believed the fairy tales. Snow White and Prince Charming. Shaun and Hannah. Happily ever after. And now its a poisoned apple. And my husband? My marriage? I want them back!

Throws frame down.

Phone rings.

HANNAH has a startled second of silence as if not knowing what to do. She jolts to reality.

Our whole lives can change in the jingle of a moment.

CHANTING

Positive. Positive. Positive. Positive. Positive.

Picks up the phone.

Shaun. Honey? What did they say?

Can we do anything? Lower the bid maybe?

No. No. I know you did. I know. Hours and hours working the numbers. I'm just…

We'll figure something else…

Just come home. Okay?

Let's grab your fishing pole. We can take a long drive, head to the river. We haven't done that in ages.

But that doesn't cost anything.

I…I don't know what else to do.

Shaun? Shaun?

Dial tone. HANNAH stares at phone. PAUSE before she hangs it up.

HANNAH slowly turns a pleading gaze direct to the audience. She struggles.

You have to be positive. Collective positive.

Are you listening? Do you get it?

We can't all give up.

Maybe *you* can turn the poisoned apple into happily ever after.

HANNAH removes the photograph of SHAUN and her from the frame. If projected, SHAUN alone fades from image. HANNAH gestures in a way that removes SHAUN from the picture - perhaps rubbing, tearing, kissing. She wraps frame in paper, pulls the box from behind the chair, and places frame in the box. She then takes another frame and does the same thing. Over and over she removes photos, wraps frames in newspaper, boxes frame.

As she does this HANNAH starts with a small laugh. It gets big, bold, shaking her body. HANNAH'S laugh rises to the level of craziness...then soft sobs as HANNAH hugs herself.

Stage lights slowly fade. If image is projected, it remains, along with sobbing.

END OF PLAY

Full Length

THE QUADROON AND THE DOVE

CHARACTERS
(In order of appearance)

SAGE-FEMME: Age 60 in Prologue. Age 75, thereafter. African ancestry. She is a sage female who comes to this from the wisdom of having lived both as a slave and as a free woman.

CLARICE: Age 16 in Prologue. Age 31, thereafter. Quadroon: very light-skinned, almost white. Haitian ancestry. She is beautiful but in this society she is considered old at age 31. She holds a position of power but doesn't truly trust the world she lives in.

ELLIE: Age 30 in Prologue. Age 45, thereafter. African ancestry. She is pragmatic, sure of her world and how best it can be lived for herself and those she loves. She holds secrets that allow her, at times, the freedom to be brazen.

JULIET: Age 15, days before her 16th birthday. Very light-skinned, almost white young woman. African ancestry. She is exceptionally beautiful, just developing the perky body of a woman, bubbly of personality, yet has that underlying current of a teenager who wants to control her destiny.

LUCIEN: Age 45. French Creole Caucasian man. Clarice and Dove's patron. Strikingly handsome, controlled, speaks with refinement. He is the master of his world yet the one thing he needs to perpetuate his line, a child, eludes him.

CHARLIE-SMITH: Age 35. Handsome, dark-skinned, muscular, large man. African ancestry. He speaks with conviction but is easily swayed by his love for Clarice.

TWO FEMALE AFRICAN DRUMMERS: Can be played by same actors as Sage-femme and Clarice disguised with masks.

CHARACTER NOTE

Quadroon was an historically racial category of hypo-descent used to describe African, Haitian, Dominican ancestry of mixed-race people in the slave societies of parts of the 19th century Louisiana. Quadroon usually referred to someone of one-quarter black ancestry.

TIME

Prologue–January 14, 1825

ACT I–January 7–9, 1841

ACT II–January 9, 1841

PLACE

New Orleans, Louisiana

SETTING

The drawing room of an 1800s Creole townhouse. The set holds a settee, desk, bar, mirror. Two new daguerreotype photographs sit on the desk: one of Juliet, one of Clarice.

At stage left a set of stairs leads to a door before a small platform representing a roof highlighted by a single roof dormer with a broken window. Half-way up the stairs is another landing leading to the bedrooms of the home. An ornate bed, representing Clarice's bedroom, is set on the landing. At stage right is an exit to the courtyard. Up stage holds a window looking out on the courtyard.

The stairs, walls, window, roof could be sturdy framed as representations but not solid walls.

At downstage left is an actor's area which changes scenes as needed.

In ACT II the Quadroon Ballroom could be achieved with light and sounds or as a full stage ornate ballroom of the era. To enhance the ball, extras may be used as dancing couples. The extras can also be used to enhance the dancing at Congo Square in ACT II.

PROLOGUE

TIME: January 14, 1825. Sunset

A slow African drum beat is heard, soft at first then rising as amber candle light illuminates far downstage left. The rest of the stage is dark. A single, stark wooden bed with a thin mattress faces upstage and holds a young ELLIE, never fully revealed to audience. CLARICE sits on the edge of the bed. Next to the bed is a small shelf with various aged bottles, one marked belladonna, and a small burlap wrapped gun. SAGE-FEMME, smoking a cigar, sings to beat of the drum.

SAGE-FEMME: (sings)

> Deep in the bayou
> When child is born,

And secrets silence
The pact is sworn.
Women lie
With men forlorn,
Hearts and bodies
Lay tattered torn.
You best be watchin'
Take care, no scorn
Cuz shrouded bonds
Bring much to mourn.

Drum fades out. ELLIE screams. CLARICE rises, crosses to SAGE-FEMME.

CLARICE: Please do something.

SAGE-FEMME: *Vous la soignez?* You care for her?

CLARICE: Of course I do. I brought her to you so she can have the best care.

SAGE-FEMME: You know that well yourself.

SAGE-FEMME crushes out cigar, kneels between ELLIE'S legs. CLARICE holds ELLIE'S hand.

SAGE-FEMME: Push.

CLARICE: You can do this. I'm right here with you.

SAGE-FEMME: That's it. Breath and scream.

CLARICE: I'll scream with you if it will help.

SAGE-FEMME: Push your baby into the world. *Bon. Bon.* I see... *pieds? Arrête. Arrête.* No more pushing. *Le bébé est renversé.* She turn. Feet first.

ELLIE: Need to push.

SAGE-FEMME: No. I try to turn.

ELLIE screams. CLARICE screams with her.

SAGE-FEMME: Must turn *bébé* or both to die.

CLARICE: You're hurting her.

SAGE-FEMME: Now. Push. Push.

> *ELLIE screams. PAUSE. A baby cries.*

CLARICE: Did you? Is she?

ELLIE: (weakly) My baby.

SAGE-FEMME: *Une fille. Une fille blanche.*

CLARICE: How can she be white?

ELLIE: (weakly) Give me my baby.

> *SAGE-FEMME wraps bundle, places it in ELLIE'S arms.*

ELLIE: (weakly) It a miracle. She have better life than me.

> *SAGE-FEMME motions CLARICE from bed.*

SAGE-FEMME: She not survive delivery. She bleeds.

CLARICE: Make it stop. (beat) Do something. Please.

SAGE-FEMME: I try, but…destiny.

ELLIE: (weakly) Clarice.

CLARICE: I am here.

ELLIE: (weakly) Promise me if anything happens to me…

SAGE-FEMME: Don't speak. Save your strength.

ELLIE: Promise…

CLARICE: Promise?

ELLIE: Promise me you take her as your own. As I've taken care of you since you was a baby.

CLARICE: You can't ask me to do that.

ELLIE: Must ask.

CLARICE: I...I cannot. I am in *plaçage* with Lucien for just a year now. He knows I was not with child.

ELLIE: She will be your niece.

CLARICE: You're a slave. I am free.

ELLIE: She white enough to pass for Quadroon.

CLARICE: He will put me out if he discovers.

ELLIE: If I tell your secret, you be put out for sure.

PAUSE

ELLIE: Raise her as your blood. No matter what happens to me. Give her your life. A Quadroon. *Une libre femme de couleur.* Free woman of color.

CLARICE: I cannot give her *my* life.

ELLIE: Then train her to own her own shop. It the best *ma bébé* can have. *Promettez moi.* Promise me.

SAGE-FEMME: She must save strength.

CLARICE: Will she live?

SAGE-FEMME: I don't know.

ELLIE weakly pushes the bundle into CLARICE'S arms. Drum best begins again. SAGE-FEMME SINGS

SAGE-FEMME: (sings)

> Deep in the bayou
> When child is born,
> And secrets silence
> The pact is sworn.

Lights and drum beat fade.

ACT I, Scene 1

TIME: *January 7, 1841*

LIGHTS UP in amber candlelight on the drawing room of LUCIEN's Creole Townhouse. The old bed and shelf have been removed. CLARICE enters, crosses to mirror, admires herself. JULIET enters, rushes to CLARICE, hugs her from behind, covers her eyes.

JULIET: Aunt Clarice!

CLARICE: Silly girl.

JULIET: I have a surprise.

CLARICE: And what might that be?

JULIET: Do you really want to see?

CLARICE: You will have to uncover my eyes.

JULIET: Ready?

CLARICE: Ready.

> *JULIET uncovers CLARICE'S eyes. She spins around.*

JULIET: Ellie is helping me. It isn't quite finished yet but she says we can get it done in time for me to watch - -

CLARICE: Oh. My. Look at you.

JULIET: Grown-up! I know. Isn't it exciting?

CLARICE: You're all a glow.

JULIET: Do you remember your first grown-up dress?

CLARICE: Mother had it made for the Quadroon Ball when she presented me in *plaçage* to Lucien.

JULIET: That was forever ago. Before I was born.

CLARICE: In some ways it feels like yesterday. And then again…

PAUSE as CLARICE inspects her face in the mirror.

JULIET: And then again?

CLARICE: We danced all night.

CLARICE takes JULIET'S hands, spins her around the room.

CLARICE: What about the dress I bought you, Juliet. I think it is appropriate for your age and you look just as beautiful.

JULIET: I want to wear this one. I'm making it as my first grown-up dress. Look, I even have a little…look.

JULIET stops dancing and points to her cleavage.

JULIET: Ellie says I'm the best seamstress she has ever seen.

CLARICE: That is what we have been striving for.

CLARICE exits to the bedroom.

JULIET: And if I have to sew all day long at least I can wear what I want.

CLARICE: (off-stage) You should try them on, side-by-side, and then we can decide.

JULIET: I don't wanna.

CLARICE enters carrying a plain, simple, cotton dress with a high neckline.

CLARICE: Please stop talking like that.

JULIET: Like what?

ELLIE enters from courtyard, carrying ribbons and sewing items.

CLARICE: Don't wanna. You sound like - -

ELLIE: She sound likes herself.

CLARICE: She sounds like those dancers in the square.

JULIET: How do you know? You've never been to Congo Square.

CLARICE: In the day, dear child. In the day.

JULIET: Come with me and Ellie next time, Aunt Clarice. I love dancing there.

CLARICE: Of course you do. You are young. But it is not a place for you, Juliet.

JULIET: Why not?

CLARICE: You and I should be above that sort of *fun*.

ELLIE: Come here, *bébé*, we finish your dress.

JULIET: Then can we go to Congo Square to dance?

CLARICE: Juliet.

JULIET: Please!

ELLIE: *Quel ruban aimerez-vous?*

JULIET: I want the blue ribbon I sewed this morning.

CLARICE: (holding up the plain dress) She really should wear this dress. It is lovely and will compliment your eyes.

ELLIE: (chuckles) I left it in my room.

JULIET: I'll...I mean I will get it.

CLARICE: You should not to go into the...Ellie's quarters. You know better than that.

JULIET: I'm only visiting just like always.

ELLIE: You kind to do so.

CLARICE: Juliet. Just because you have been doing something for a long time does not make it right. Ellie will please get the

141

ribbon and discourage you from visiting her room and accompanying her to Congo Square.

ELLIE: (chuckles) You know I take her anyplace she want to go.

CLARICE: You should not go to certain places that can be dangerous.

ELLIE: Nothing gonna happen when she's with me. You look at yourself in the pretty mirror.

ELLIE exits via courtyard as both JULIET and CLARICE look at their reflections.

CLARICE: Do you think you are being a bit willful?

JULIET: Because I am friends with Ellie and Charlie-Smith?

CLARICE: They are your slaves. Not your friends.

JULIET: You're friendly with Charlie-Smith.

CLARICE: What do you mean?

JULIET: You talk with him when he brushes Sunny. I've seen you.

CLARICE: Yes. Of course. I am being cordial. I must...care for them. Mister Lucien expects it of me. And I expect you to behave like a proper girl and wear the dress I bought you.

JULIET: But, Mister Lucien will love this dress.

CLARICE: It should not matter what he thinks.

JULIET: He brought me chocolate the other day.

CLARICE: He brings chocolates to all of us, child. Trust me, it is really for his own sweet tooth. I certainly cannot eat too much and stay, well, and fit into my ball gown.

JULIET: If you get fat I can let all your dresses out.

CLARICE: Thank you. I think. (beat) Juliet, my fondest hope for you is be, as you say, the best seamstress and one day open your own shop.

JULIET: That's all you want for me?

CLARICE: I want you to have freedoms that I never had.

JULIET: You have everything because Mister Lucian takes care of you.

CLARICE: (looks in mirror, inspecting) Is that what you think?

JULIET nods.

CLARICE: I'm sure the world looks just that black and white to you but it is not that simple.

JULIET: I think I'm old enough to make my own choices. To have fun and be pretty. There is nothing wrong with that.

CLARICE: No, dear child, of course not. You should want to have fun and be pretty but you must also trust that I know what is best for you. And, will be here for you as long as you listen to me.

JULIET: Can I listen to you say yes?

CLARICE: (chuckles) You are headstrong.

JULIET takes CLARICE'S hands and dances her around the room.

CLARICE: Look how happy you are.

JULIET: We'll have fun.

ELLIE enters, makes herself busy with sewing items. CLARICE and JULIET stop dancing.

CLARICE: Very well. You may wear the dress you made but only if you have a little less...

CLARICE points to JULIET'S cleavage and smiles.

JULIET: And you'll come dance with us in the square? Give up. Say yes.

CLARICE: I never give up on what I want. (beat) Ellie, did you fix that dormer window, yet?

JULIET: I can help.

CLARICE: As I have said many times, the roof is not the place for a girl to be playing.

JULIET: I don't play. I read. I watch the city. It's quiet up there.

CLARICE: It is dangerous.

ELLIE: It be peaceful.

JULIET: It is.

CLARICE: Ellie please fix the dormer without Juliet's help.

ELLIE: I measure it later.

CLARICE: Get Charlie-Smith to cut you some wood to cover it for now. And the ball is in two days so please mend my light pink cape.

JULIET: Wear the blue one and we can share the ribbon.

CLARICE: Light pink brightens my skin.

ELLIE: I get it soon as I finish this here dress for li'l Dove.

LUCIEN enters with a smile that lights up the room. JULIET rushes to LUCIEN who twirls her around.

LUCIEN: My. My.

CLARICE: Be careful.

LUCIEN: Where is that little girl Dove?

JULIET: What little girl, Mister Lucien?

LUCIEN: You are growing into a young lady right before my eyes.

JULIET: It's the dress. Do you like it?

LUCIEN: (sets Juliet down) I do. But, I think, no, it is more than that.

ELLIE: She gonna be a proper young lady.

LUCIEN: Your Aunt Clarice was your age when we entered *plaçage*. Sixteen. And just as beautiful.

JULIET: Sixteen years, almost exactly.

LUCIEN: One week.

JULIET: What will you give me?

CLARICE: Juliet. You should not be so bold.

LUCIEN: Why not? You were bold at sixteen and you still are, *ma chère*.

CLARICE: And you are still a charmer, Lucien. I have a surprise for you.

CLARICE takes a small box from the desk, hands it to LUCIEN, he opens it.

LUCIEN: A compass.

CLARICE: So you can always find your way to me. I had Mr. Barbé craft it especially with an ivory case and a flourish 'L' for your name in mother-of-pearl.

LUCIEN kisses & hugs CLARICE.

LUCIEN: You do spoil me. But, then again, you have had years of experience with me, haven't you?

CLARICE: Many years of love.

LUCIEN: *Oui.* So how much did the love of a compass cost me?

CLARICE: I paid for it myself.

LUCIEN: Ever since your mother presented you to me at the ball, you have been a clever girl in making the most of your allowance. And in pleasing me. Even after all these years you sometimes look like the young girl I brought to this house.

CLARICE: Only sometimes?

LUCIEN: If I tell you *all* the time you will get lazy and then, well…I fear you would not fare well on your own as a dressmaker, cook, or as a shop girl.

JULIET: Why would that happen?

CLARICE: It won't. Ever.

LUCIEN: That would be the fate of a *placée* if she were to be put out or if her protector died.

CLARICE: You will never die.

LUCIEN: Not with you about to keep me happy.

JULIET: You two should get married.

ELLIE: Dove. Hush.

JULIET: It doesn't make sense that you can't be together.

CLARICE: Sometimes it doesn't make sense to me either.

LUCIEN: Dove, you have lived in this home all your life. Surely you have some understanding of *plaçage*. Your aunt is Quadroon, one-quarter negro, three-quarters - -

CLARICE: White.

LUCIEN: Mixed blood, as are you.

JULIET: If you love her and she loves you then the color of your skin shouldn't matter.

LUCIEN: The rules of society are complicated. I am a native-born French Creole. Because your aunt is not pure, we cannot marry.

CLARICE: That is not always true, though, is it? Some native Creole men have married their *placée*.

LUCIEN: And they have been ostracized.

CLARICE: In New Orleans, perhaps, but not everywhere.

LUCIEN: New Orleans is our *world*. And allows certain privileges that are attained, encouraged even, as long as they are kept within proper parameters for every gentleman. My wife? In my mansion on St. Charles Avenue. My...Clarice? Here on Rue Rampart. It was so with my father, and his father, and is so for me. In *plaçage*, I provide my little Clarice this home and an allowance. And I love her. In return, she is devoted to me.

CLARICE: Eternally.

LUCIEN: As am I.

CLARICE: We could leave New Orleans. Go away together.

LUCIEN: Only in your dreams. Dove, *plaçage* is a magical arrangement. It begins with the ball where Quadroons are chosen by Native Creole men like me. You feel like...Cinderella, didn't you, *ma chère*?

CLARICE: Those would not be my words, Lucien. But Juliet is too young to hear these intricacies.

JULIET: Why do you think it is wrong that I am curious about life? I'm almost sixteen.

CLARICE: It is not wrong but your life is set. You will have the best dress shop in New Orleans which will come with freedoms I cannot have - -

LUCIEN: Are you not free?

ELLIE motions JULIET to the fitting.

CLARICE: What?

LUCIEN: Are you unhappy with your life?

CLARICE: No. Of course not. I am happy. It is just that Juliet's path to happiness will be - -

LUCIEN: More free?

CLARICE: Lucien, you are twisting my words.

LUCIEN: First you have no freedom and now I am manipulating you. Perhaps your mother should have trained *you* to be a seamstress instead of my *placée*.

CLARICE: I am exactly where I want to be. With you.

LUCIEN: As it should be. You have always been the clever girl.

CLARICE: Yes. Well, now I am setting Juliet's life as her aunt.

LUCIEN: You mean, of course, that I am setting her life and making decisions for both of you, as always.

CLARICE: I simply meant that her freedoms will be different.

JULIET: You want me to be an old maid stuck here until I die.

CLARICE: That is not - -

LUCIEN: Dove you could no more be an old maid than you could a slave.

ELLIE: Dove, you want some feathers on your dress?

JULIET nods.

ELLIE: Blue or white.

LUCIEN: White.

ELLIE: I be right back.

ELLIE looks at CLARICE and exits.

LUCIEN: How are your studies going?

CLARICE: Ellie says she is a very good seamstress.

LUCIEN: Good. And is that all you are studying?

JULIET: No.

CLARICE: No?

JULIET: Please do not be angry with me.

LUCIEN: Of course not. Opening one's mind is never a bad thing.

JULIET: I've been reading.

CLARICE: On the roof?

JULIET: Every chance I get. All those books in Mister Lucien's library.

LUCIEN: It is good that *someone* is using them. So, tell me, what are your favorites?

JULIET: Anything about history. And architecture. I love thinking about the past and the present and the future.

LUCIEN: How so?

JULIET: Last year, the twenty-fifth anniversary of the Battle of New Orleans, we celebrated the past, present, and future when President Jackson laid the cornerstone for his monument at *Place d'Armes*.

LUCIEN: You have been learning. *Bon. Bon.* We should go for a ride along the river tomorrow. You can come with me to inspect my ships and then I will walk you around *Place d'Armes* while we talk history and architecture.

CLARICE: That will be fun.

LUCIEN: I will take Dove alone. As her birthday gift.

CLARICE: But we can all enjoy - -

LUCIEN: No. No need. It will feed into her readings. Then we will enjoy dinner at Antoine's.

JULIET: Antoine's! Oh I have wanted to go there since it opened last year. Aunt Clarice said it was a grown-up place.

LUCIEN: It is. But I think you are ready. *Oui.* Then off to my box at *Théâtre d'Orléans* to see *Mademoiselle Julie Calvé.* Would you like that?

JULIET: Very much.

ELLIE enters with feathers.

CLARICE: She will have to be in by nine o'clock. The laws, Lucien.

LUCIEN: Not if she is with me.

CLARICE: Ellie. Why don't you take Juliet back to her room and finish the dress.

LUCIEN: *Reste ici.* I love watching the fitting.

CLARICE: Lucien, I thought we would take a walk.

ELLIE: Charlie-Smith say you gonna visit him, go for a ride on Sunny.

CLARICE: (nervously) I never said - -

ELLIE: He say he be waiting for you, like always.

LUCIEN: If you would rather ride.

CLARICE: No. I would rather walk with you.

LUCIEN: I love our walks. Yes. A walk to the river and back to watch the sunset on your face. We could run my courses. I need cigars from George Alces and Mr. Legoaster should be done with my riding coat, and a copy of the *Picayune.*

CLARICE: That will be lovely.

LUCIEN: You know the shops.

CLARICE: All your favorites. Only the best. We should go now so as not to lose the light.

LUCIEN: You are the clever girl, thinking about the time. Perhaps you should run my courses first, then we shall walk. Isn't that the smart thing to do?

CLARICE: Together will be more fun.

LUCIEN: If you go now and get back quick as a bunny, we will still enjoy a lovely walk together. Don't forget to put your *chignon* on your head. I would hate for my wife to see you uncovered and have you arrested.

CLARICE, haltingly, crosses to courtyard exit, takes chignon and begins wrapping her head. She exits while looking back at the JULIET, ELLIE and LUCIEN.

LUCIEN: Ellie, this dress is pretty but Dove needs something more elaborate.

ELLIE: She only gonna be watch people in it, Mister Lucien.

LUCIEN: She is representing me and my household. And I say it needs change.

Lights fade.

ACT I, Scene 2

TIME: *January 7, 1841. Later that same evening*

Gloaming LIGHTS UP as ELLIE, wrapped in a warm coat, is seen on the roof, working on cleaning the debris from the window of the dormer. She finishes, turns, pulls on door to open: it doesn't budge. ELLIE struggles. CHARLIE-SMITH enters via the courtyard.

CHARLIE-SMITH: (quietly) Clarice. You be in here? Clarice.

CHARLIE-SMITH crosses to the stairs.

Clarice?

He crosses to landing, peeks towards bedroom.

That you? I was waiting at the stable. You never come down. Thought we was gonna - -

ELLIE: Is someone there? (bangs on door) *Ouvrez!* Let me in! It be freezing out here. Hello!

CHARLIE-SMITH rises to roof, opens door.

'Bout time. I was soon to catch my death out there in this January cold. (beat) What you doin' in the house?

CHARLIE-SMITH: Saving your life.

ELLIE: Hmm. (beat) *Oui.* Where was you last night?

CHARLIE-SMITH: No where.

ELLIE: Don't be lying to me, Charlie-Smith.

CHARLIE-SMITH: I was…in the barn…shoeing Miss Clarice's Sunny.

ELLIE: That's a bold faced lie. She was planning on riding Sunny this afternoon and if you'd'a just shoed her you woulda said she take another horse.

CHARLIE-SMITH: Well, she didn't even show so - -

ELLIE: No?

CHARLIE-SMITH: No.

ELLIE: Hmm. But you still be lying to me. Where you go?

CHARLIE-SMITH: Congo Square to dance.

ELLIE: You left your room long past midnight.

CHARLIE-SMITH: Where I go is none of your business.

ELLIE: I know where ya was and you be getting us all in trouble iffin' you don't stop this nonsense.

CHARLIE-SMITH: We can't live like this no more.

ELLIE: We get lots more than some. Mister Lucien gives us rooms not falling in, food on the table, nights to dance at the Square.

CHARLIE-SMITH: They take away our rights for freedom, Ellie. Sage-femme was freed when I's a teenager. Mister Lucien freed her hisself.

ELLIE: Was easier back then. No money, no curfew, no rules on testifying in court or printing things in the newspaper. Even Clarice and Dove, doesn't seem to matter they free. They still has to follow laws.

CHARLIE-SMITH: Laws that didn't be existing before eleven years ago.

ELLIE: They find it as insulting as we does.

CHARLIE-SMITH: It not fair. We got to fight.

ELLIE: You watch what you saying in this house, you hear me. Mister Lucien be hearing you talk such and he be selling you to the first Georgia plantation he finds. You want that?

CHARLIE-SMITH: I want my chance to be free.

ELLIE: Mister Lucien ain't gonna post no one thousand dollar bond if you free to guarantee you leave Louisiana in thirty days. You born a slave. You die a slave. Just likes me.

CHARLIE-SMITH: I want the chance Sage-femme had. The chance my mama and papa had. What happening to New Orleans when we ain't even got a chance to be free people of color?

ELLIE: You don't need to be worrying about what happening beyond this house and these people. They your...your...

CHARLIE-SMITH: Master.

ELLIE: And mistress, lest you be forgetting that part.

CHARLIE-SMITH: I never forgetting that.

ELLIE: You fight. You run. Things change with her, too. You think of that?

PAUSE as CHARLIE-SMITH considers.

ELLIE: Put that fighting nonsense out your head. It ain't gonna happen. Come on down to the kitchen and I get you some supper. Then you cut me a heavy piece of wood to cover up that hole until the glass maker get to it.

ELLIE exits via the courtyard. CHARLIE-SMITH stays, trying to control his anger.

Lights fade.

ACT I, Scene 3

TIME: January 8, 1841. The next evening.

Sparkling LIGHTS UP downstage left on a finely set table of Antoine's restaurant. The rest of the stage remains dark. The same melody that accompanied SAGE-FEMME'S singing, is heard. LUCIEN and JULIET, finely dressed, sit at the table.

JULIET: The ride along the river was glorious. All those steamboats, there must have been hundreds of them!

LUCIEN: Our port is busier than that of New York. Did you like *my* steamboats?

JULIET: I did. I mean I would. But I don't know how to tell, exactly, which are yours and which aren't…are not, I mean.

LUCIEN: No need to be so formal with me, Dove. Your enthusiasm is genuine. You're like a breath of ocean breeze floating up the Mississippi, drowning out the ills of the city. (beat) My ships have the Boudet Crest, a yellow background with a Pegasus in the center.

JULIET: A winged horse?

LUCIEN: A majestic winged horse. Although I think our horses today could have outrun even a Pegasus.

JULIET: I think you're right.

LUCIEN: *T'aime le champagne, chèrie?*

JULIET: It's delicious but I might have had too much. I'm feeling a bit silly.

LUCIEN: A girl your age should feel silly with her first sip of champagne but, perhaps you have had enough.

JULIET: I have a confession. It is not my first sip. Ellie was making *poulet au champagne* a while back and I, well, I snuck a glass out of the kitchen.

LUCIEN: (laughing) Clever girl.

JULIET: You won't tell Aunt Clarice, will you?

LUCIEN: It will be our secret. What shall we conspire next? Caviar?

JULIET: Secret caviar? Doesn't sound as fun as secret champagne.

LUCIEN: You mean you haven't snuck any out of Ellie's kitchen?

JULIET: Aunt Clarice says caviar is too expensive. It sounds a bit distasteful to me, eating fish eggs.

LUCIEN: Let's try and you can tell me what you think.

LUCIEN picks up a small spoon of caviar and moves to hand the spoon to JULIET.

For you.

JULIET takes his hand and guides the caviar into her mouth.

(flustered) Oh. Well. Yes. Well. *Bon, non?*

JULIET: (nodding) Maybe you can sneak some into the house for me. Then we *can* have secret caviar.

LUCIEN: (flustered) Yes. Well. Perhaps. Or not.

JULIET: Why not? It could be a game, our little secrets.

LUCIEN: Too many secrets might not be good.

JULIET: How can champagne and caviar be bad? I want to enjoy this every day.

LUCIEN: (recovering) I don't think we can live at Antoine's.

JULIET: We could steal away in one of the upstairs club rooms. And play hide and seek.

LUCIEN: Where would you hide first?

JULIET: They say there are secret rooms only for wealthy gentlemen to enjoy their absinthe and cigars. I should like to hide in them to see what really goes on.

LUCIEN: And what if they found you? *Alors?*

JULIET: I would stand my ground and tell them to give me an absinthe.

LUCIEN: (laughing) They would not stand a chance against you.

JULIET: Unless they were old and scary. Then I would run!

LUCIEN: Delightful.

JULIET: And you'd protect me.

LUCIEN: As I protect your aunt.

JULIET: But it would be different.

LUCIEN: How so?

JULIET: I would be just a seamstress.

LUCIEN: Perhaps. (beat) Dove? Are you enjoying your birthday celebration?

JULIET: More than any ever before. Ever.

LUCIEN: You are growing up.

JULIET: I'm *grown* up.

LUCIEN: And getting educated. It is time we thought of your future.

JULIET: Aunt Clarice has me sewing all day long, except when I sneak up to the roof.

LUCIEN: Clever girl.

JULIET: She's been inquiring about a position in one of the dress-making shops.

LUCIEN: She has?

JULIET: One day I'll own a shop of my own.

LUCIEN: You are *une libre femme de couleur*, free to work as a seamstress and then, yes, open your own shop. As an unattached woman, that is the highest you could hope to attain.

JULIET: Would you visit me in my shop?

LUCIEN: I would.

JULIET: And buy dresses for Aunt Clarice?

LUCIEN: And my wife.

JULIET: You would keep me busy.

LUCIEN: True. But I think we should strive for more, don't you?

JULIET: All of my reading has opened my eyes to so much. I know I could never hope for it but I want to go to Paris and study.

LUCIEN: Or you could be bold and go simply for the pleasures of the city.

JULIET: A single young lady alone in Paris? Scandalous.

LUCIEN: You wouldn't have to be alone.

JULIET: Promise?

LUCIEN: I could find you a suitable traveling companion.

JULIET: Oh. Who?

LUCIEN: I will think on it. *Et après Paris?*

JULIET: Aunt Clarice wants me to stay with her.

LUCIEN: You certainly could stay forever, as you are, with your aunt, but do you want more?

JULIET: Is it awful that I do?

LUCIEN: You could...if you so choose...be presented at the Quadroon Ball for *plaçage.*

JULIET: Aunt Clarice said I can only go to watch the ball tomorrow night. I can't be presented.

LUCIEN: Why?

JULIET: She says it wouldn't be proper.

LUCIEN: She is mistaken. Your aunt was presented at your age. (beat) Oh, back then, the balls were *plentiful* and *extravagant.* Months of planning and the highlight of the season. And now? Just this one. (beat) If you so desire...

JULIET: I don't want to be willful. I'm grateful to have a place in Aunt Clarice's house.

LUCIEN: *My* house.

JULIET: Yes, your house.

LUCIEN: You can have your own home on Rue Rampart.

JULIET: With a roof where I can sit and read and watch the city?

LUCIEN: (chuckling) A roof with a Dove perch.

JULIET: Maybe a whole coop.

LUCIEN: For you and your little doves?

JULIET: If I were in *plaçage,* I would travel the world and study.

LUCIEN: And after that?

JULIET: Does that have to end?

LUCIEN: A home would be expected.

JULIET: Then I would give my protector children.

LUCIEN: Children.

JULIET: Yes. I will read them all the books in the library and take them around the world with me.

LUCIEN: Children are the hope of any man but, sometimes, life has other plans. (beat) I have found great joy watching you grow into a fine young lady. You are clever, bold, lovely. Any Creole would take pleasure in spoiling you. You would have slaves to tend to your every - -

JULIET: I wouldn't want that.

LUCIEN: What?

JULIET: Slaves. I would free them.

LUCIEN: That would be an expensive proposition.

JULIET: You don't think the repressive laws are fair, do you?

LUCIEN: We have been enduring the American for decades yet they make no effort to understand our culture or ways. With our slaves, properties, loves. You would decide, with your protector, how you would run the household with the allowance given you. You would find it easier with slaves.

JULIET: In a way, don't we treat the slaves like the Americans treat us? Not understanding their culture, their ways?

LUCIEN: You *do* know some of the world, Dove. It is true I was able to allow more freedom before 1830.

JULIET: Is that when Sage-femme was freed?

LUCIEN: No. I freed her a few years before you were born. It was easier to allow back then. But the Americans think every negro should be a slave. And while I certainly enjoy the privilege and tradition of slaves, our society could not function without free persons of color, like you. In any event, your protector will care for you, love you.

JULIET: Aunt Clarice won't approve.

LUCIEN: Let me worry about her. What do you want? If it is to have the best dress shop in all of New Orleans, I will see to it. But, if you want more?

JULIET: I want to taste the world.

LUCIEN: A protector could provide that and more.

JULIET: He would be kind, caring?

LUCIEN: (nods) You will find such a prince at the ball.

JULIET: No one old.

LUCIEN: (amused) I promise, no one old.

JULIET: Or too young.

LUCIEN: What is too young?

JULIET: No one my age. They're all silly.

LUCIEN: And they have no property or power.

JULIET: And no one poor.

LUCIEN: (amused) Never poor. You will be kept in style, *chèrie*.

JULIET: Not a stranger.

LUCIEN: Most *placées* do not know their protector until the ball.

JULIET: Wouldn't it be better if it were someone I already knew? I would be eternally devoted, in every way.

LUCIEN: Yes. Well. (beat) Your aunt will present you at the ball.

JULIET: Thank you. Mister Lucien.

LUCIEN: Lucien.

JULIET: What?

LUCIEN: I think it is time you called me Lucien.

JULIET: I don't know. Aunt Clarice - -

LUCIEN: Did I say I will take care of everything?

JULIET nods.

JULIET: So we have another secret?

LUCIEN: Only until tomorrow night.

Lights and music fade.

ACT I, Scene 4

TIME: *January 8, 1841. Midnight.*

LIGHTS UP in amber candlelight on the drawing room. The table has been removed. CLARICE paces. JULIET twirls excitedly into the room, humming. She stops abruptly when she sees CLARICE.

JULIET: Aunt Clarice. You surprised me. I didn't imagine you'd still be up.

CLARICE: I expected you hours ago.

JULIET: Time flew by.

CLARICE crosses to JULIET and hugs her.

CLARICE: I was worried. You could have been arrested or hi-jacked into those cribs by the river or trampled to death by a runaway horse.

JULIET: I was with Lucien.

CLARICE releases JULIET.

CLARICE: *Mister* Lucien.

JULIET: Do you want to hear about our evening?

CLARICE: Tell me all about it.

JULIET: I rode Sunny. Charlie-Smith had Dawn side-saddled for me but Lucien //

CLARICE: *Mister* Lucien.

JULIET: // insisted I have the fastest horse in the stable. After his Beacon, of course. So, I hopped right on. She is swift. I can see why you love to ride her. We raced along the river - -

CLARICE: What do you mean hopped right on? Surely Charlie-Smith had to change the saddles.

JULIET: (shaking her head 'no') I didn't ride side-saddle. I couldn't race that way. Lucien said I was bold.

CLARICE: Dear Juliet, you must maintain decorum.

JULIET: (excited) There is nothing more than the corner stone for Andrew Jackson's monument. Lucien says there is no money for it now although I hope there will be soon. Lucien says there is talk of major renovation to St. Louis Cathedral. We chattered non-stop, like my doves, as we walked around *Place d'Armes*. I think you would have enjoyed it. I would love to go back tomorrow but we won't have time.

CLARICE: Why not?

JULIET: Why, the ball, of course!

CLARICE: Of course. Perhaps the day after we can spend the afternoon together. Pampering ourselves. We could visit Sage-femme for some flowers and teas.

JULIET: You have to go to Antoine's, Aunt Clarice. It is scrumptious. Lucien says that even though they've only been open since the Spring, he can find nothing that needs improving. Oh, and we talked of everything: his business, Paris, children, law - -

CLARICE: Children? You discussed children?

JULIET: Doves, really. I said I would like a coop and he said for me and my little doves. And when I said I was going to try to sneak in to see the gentlemen's club rooms, we laughed. I am so curious about them and he said he might just sneak me in one night. Of course he has entry. Can you imagine it?

CLARICE: Lucian has entry all over the city. He is a powerful man.

JULIET: I had caviar although I don't think I like it. Don't tell Lucien, though, I wouldn't want him to think me a child.

CLARICE: Don't wish your childhood away so fast.

JULIET: I wish you would let me grow up.

CLARICE: I am letting you grow up, dear child.

JULIET: I'm not a child.

CLARICE: I want you to be a proper young lady, Juliet. Someone who has a chance to better herself. To do for herself. You cannot do that with rudeness. Lucien is your...uncle. You should address him properly.

JULIET: Why can't you let me be happy tonight? It was magical from start to finish.

CLARICE: Dear chil...Juliet. I am always happy when you beam and tomorrow you can tell me more. For tonight, I think you should go to bed, yes?

JULIET: I'm not ready.

CLARICE: I think you are.

JULIET stands defiantly.

CLARICE: Unless you want to attend the ball with puffy eyes and blotchy skin from lack of sleep.

LUCIEN enters.

JULIET: Fine. But I am going to bed because I want to, not because you say so.

LUCIEN: So early?

CLARICE: It is midnight. She should be asleep.

LUCIEN: Sweetest dreams, Dove.

163

LUCIEN crosses to JULIET and kisses her on the cheek, lingering a bit too long. JULIET smiles, turns dramatically, ascends stairs to the landing.

JULIET: I'll dream of fantasies that will come true.

JULIET exits to the bedrooms.

LUCIEN: She could have stayed up a bit longer, don't you think?

CLARICE: She is a young girl and needs her beauty sleep.

LUCIEN: She is not a girl, Clarice. And what if we were not through with our evening?

CLARICE: You were.

LUCIEN: (laughing) So transparent.

CLARICE: I have no idea what you mean.

LUCIEN crosses to CLARICE, kisses her.

LUCIEN: The night was special. Like when you and I first met. Do you remember, *ma chère*? You were young, beautiful. Devoted to me.

CLARICE: Eternally.

LUCIEN: I knew then that you were special.

LUCIEN continues to seduce her.

CLARICE: We should leave. Run to the west, to being together always.

LUCIEN: West? To Indians and mud? You would not like that society.

CLARICE: We'll start our own society. No hiding, no *chignon* on my head, no restrictions on where we could go, how we should behave. I will not have to carry identification proving I am *libérer la femme de couleur*. We would be free. Just the two of us.

LUCIEN: And what of Juliet?

CLARICE: You said yourself she is growing up. We can find a proper shop for her.

LUCIEN: She is destined for more.

CLARICE: Then the best shop in the city. And we can sell Ellie & Charlie-Smith.

LUCIEN: Why would we sell them?

CLARICE: If it were just the two of us it would be so easy. We could arrange for transport on one of your riverboats to take the two of us to *St. Louis* and from there we could go anywhere we want.

LUCIEN: Isn't all that I give you enough? This house, slaves to care for you, money to spend, freedom to roam - -

CLARICE: Only if properly covered.

LUCIEN: Is that such a hardship?

CLARICE: Why should we bear any hardship at all?

LUCIEN: I have a wife.

CLARICE: Whom you do not love.

LUCIEN: Not in the same way I love you. It is true.

CLARICE: We could have the best life, just the two of us. Juliet is perched to live her own life. Ellie and Charlie-Smith make demands. All your wife does is flounce about in her big St. Charles Street mansion throwing tea parties and being - -

LUCIEN stops seducing and looks at her.

LUCIEN: Stop. We have had this conversation too many times over the years.

CLARICE: I love you.

LUCIEN: And I you, *ma chère.*

CLARICE: As much as when I was young?

LUCIEN: Why would I not? You are aging well.

CLARICE: Aging well.

LUCIEN: *Oui.* And you have my love in the proper ways that society demands.

CLARICE: I am not enough for you.

LUCIEN: In many ways, you are enough, as you are, no more. And I have accepted you...despite your shortcomings

PAUSE

CLARICE: I am sorry.

LUCIEN: It is hurtful to you for us to visit this again, no? So let us not.

CLARICE: I wanted us to be bound with children.

LUCIEN: That was also my fondest desire. And *is* my greatest disappointment. But I still love you. I know you would do anything for me.

LUCIEN pours two drinks, hands one to CLARICE, kisses her on the cheek.

LUCIEN: You are going to present Dove at the ball.

CLARICE: I do not think - -

LUCIEN: It is not for you to think. You will present her as a mother would, and she will be taken into *plaçage*. This is best for her as it was for you.

CLARICE: It is best for her to own a shop, as she has been groomed. To live her life on her own terms.

LUCIEN: No. No. She will study in Paris. Her protector will make it so. As I did with you, *ma chère* and you came back to me more enticing than when you left.

CLARICE: That is not Juliet's destiny.

LUCIEN: It is what she wishes.

CLARICE: It is not supposed to be this way.

LUCIEN: What do you mean?

CLARICE: What?

LUCIEN: What is not supposed to be?

CLARICE: I mean…perhaps her protector would not allow this.

LUCIEN: He will. Her destiny is already in motion.

CLARICE: You spoke with her of this?

> *LUCIEN nods.*

CLARICE: And she agreed?

LUCIEN: She is excited, as long as I promise her no old men.

CLARICE: You have someone in mind.

LUCIEN: I am thinking on that. Someone suitable. Someone who will love her. Eternally.

CLARICE: She is only fifteen Lucien.

LUCIEN: Sixteen next week.

CLARICE: Too young - -

LUCIEN: That is why I am thinking, *ma chère*, because I know what is best.

> *PAUSE*

CLARICE: No, Lucien. You cannot do this. I will not allow it.

LUCIEN: *Pardon?*

CLARICE: I have raised her as my own. You strut in here when it suits you and think you know what is best for her?

CHARLIE-SMITH appears in the window.

LUCIEN: Clarice.

CLARICE: This can't happen.

LUCIEN: But it will.

CLARICE: You haven't thought this through.

LUCIEN: Are you questioning me?

CLARICE: I am only thinking of Juliet.

LUCIEN: Really?

CLARICE: Of course. As always.

LUCIEN: And, as always, you will listen to me.

CLARICE: No.

LUCIEN: I do what is best for both of you.

CLARICE: I can't allow this to happen.

LUCIEN: You can't?

CLARICE: No, Lucien. Do you hear me? No!

LUCIEN: Calm down, Clarice.

CLARICE: I know what you're planning. I know!

LUCIEN: I am planning that your niece will be happy. Isn't that what you have always wanted?

CLARICE: Not this way.

LUCIEN: You have no say.

CLARICE: I do!

LUCIEN: Clarice.

CLARICE: You won't do this!

LUCIEN: Clarice!

CLARICE: It won't happen. We'll go west - -

LUCIEN strikes CLARICE. CHARLIE-SMITH rushes in. LUCIEN turns, looks at him with authority. CHARLIE-SMITH stops.

LUCIEN: (to Charlie-Smith) What?

PAUSE

CHARLIE-SMITH: (fuming but forced to remember his place) You.

LUCIEN: Yes. Me. Master of this household.

LUCIEN turns to CLARICE.

Eternally devoted. You will believe that. I shall see you at the ball and Dove will be properly presented. Until then, I hope you think about your place.

LUCIEN throws back his drink, kisses CLARICE on the forehead, stares one second at CHARLIE-SMITH, and exits.

CHARLIE-SMITH: When he hit you, I want to kill him.

CLARICE: You would be hung.

CHARLIE-SMITH: There be places to hide a body in the bayou.

CLARICE: That must never happen. I have sacrificed to build my life and it can't be destroyed. By you. By Juliet. By anyone.

CHARLIE-SMITH: He doesn't love you like I do. You have me. Have always had me. I do anything for you. Clarice. I take you west.

CLARICE: What?

CHARLIE-SMITH: You be wanting to get away from New Orleans. I run away with you.

CLARICE: You are a slave, Charlie-Smith.

CHARLIE-SMITH: You free me.

CLARICE: Only Lucien can free you.

CHARLIE-SMITH: We be doin' this. Go west, like you want.

CLARICE: I wish it were that easy.

CHARLIE-SMITH: But you said - -

CLARICE: You do not understand.

CHARLIE-SMITH: We can make our life together.

CLARICE: Stop. Please. You are talking as crazy as Lucien. You and I can never leave here. I can never leave without Lucien. This life. This position I have. It all comes because I love him.

CHARLIE-SMITH: You love me.

CLARICE: It is different.

CHARLIE-SMITH: I share your bed when Mister Lucien is with his wife and I accept bein' in the dark cuz that what you want. But what you say to him can be us. We can have a life out west. If not...

CLARICE: It is not that simple. You can never give me what I have here. You're Negro.

CHARLIE-SMITH: You be Negro.

ELLIE enters, unseen by CLARICE and CHARLIE-SMITH.

CLARICE: We are not the same. I need Lucien. I need you both. Why must you torment me?

CHARLIE-SMITH: My love be true. But you be...blind. And so was I. But I can't be no more. I will be free. With you or without you.

ELLIE: You best be watching yourself. What if I was Mister Lucien who enter just now? What then?

CHARLIE-SMITH: What then, Clarice?

CLARICE: I do not think he would care.

ELLIE: You bein' foolish.

CHARLIE-SMITH: Maybe I bein' foolish.

CHARLIE-SMITH exits via courtyard.

CLARICE: I just want some peace.

ELLIE: Peace for who?

CLARICE and ELLIE stare at each other.

Lights fade.

ACT I, Scene 5

TIME: January 9, 1841. Sunrise. The day of the Quadroon Ball.

Amber candle light illuminate far downstage left. The rest of the stage is dark. SAGE-FEMME, smoking a cigar and humming to a drum beat, stands beside her bed and shelf. CHARLIE-SMITH drinks a cup of tea from a huge tattered mug.

CHARLIE-SMITH: I pulled in two ways, to freedom and to her.

SAGE-FEMME: Drink your tea and then we read the leaves. *Nous trouvons la vérité.* We find truth for war and love, no?

CHARLIE-SMITH: The meeting's are heat and venom. Men bein' denied our rights.

SAGE-FEMME: You gonna rise up?

CHARLIE-SMITH: Don't have no choice. Laws unfair. They take away our chances to be free.

SAGE-FEMME: Even poor free, like me, better than a slave.

CHARLIE-SMITH: Why didn't you leave? Go north all those years ago?

SAGE-FEMME: I woulda had to hide, even traveling with papers. Some men only see what they want, despite what in front of them. Here? Everybody know I a freed woman.

CHARLIE-SMITH: I'd never stay if I was free.

SAGE-FEMME: And if Clarice says you stay with her. Stay a slave. What you do then, eh?

CHARLIE-SMITH shakes his head.

SAGE-FEMME: You best be figuring it out. Once you make the choice, no easy thing to go back. Finish and spit in the cup. We see where your future lie.

CHARLIE-SMITH finishes his tea, spits in the cup, gingerly places the cup in SAGE-FEMME'S hand.

CHARLIE-SMITH: Tell me what to do.

SAGE-FEMME: The leaves guide you. I just read what destiny already written.

PAUSE as SAGE-FEMME turns the mug.

SAGE-FEMME: I see much. The nail intertwined with an ax and hammer. You suffer an injustice, you must work hard to overcome.

CHARLIE-SMITH nods. SAGE-FEMME turns the mug.

SAGE-FEMME: I sees a heart.

CHARLIE-SMITH: Clarice?

SAGE-FEMME: The heart rests by a lamp. Secrets to be revealed about this loved one but there is also a fork so beware of false flattery.

CHARLIE-SMITH: How I know what be false?

SAGE-FEMME: Look for the lamp.

CHARLIE-SMITH: What lamp?

SAGE-FEMME: A lamp that will light the way.

SAGE-FEMME turns the mug.

SAGE-FEMME: I see a closed bag tied with a wavy line. A trap, a uncertain path. *Prends garde.*

CHARLIE-SMITH: Beware of what? Of who? I more confused than before.

SAGE-FEMME: No. You more aware. Be keen. Sharp. Don't be swayed by falsehoods. Trust yourself before all others.

SAGE-FEMME crosses to shelf, retrieves the burlap wrapped gun. She unwraps it and holds it out to CHARLIE-SMITH.

CHARLIE-SMITH: What I need this for?

SAGE-FEMME: Protect yourself.

SAGE-FEMME puts the gun in his hand.

CHARLIE-SMITH: You didn't tell me which path to be takin'.

SAGE-FEMME: You will know, *dans ton coeur.*

CHARLIE-SMITH: My heart?

SAGE-FEMME: Listen to your heart. It will tell you when the time be right.

The sound of an approaching horse is heard. CLARICE enters at a run.

CLARICE: Sage-femme. I need to...Charlie-Smith? (beat) What are you doing here?

CHARLIE-SMITH crosses to CLARICE.

CHARLIE-SMITH: Is my love torment?

CLARICE looks nervously at SAGE-FEMME.

SAGE-FEMME: I leave you alone, for a bit. Charlie-Smith, remember all the tea leaves say, all I give you.

SAGE-FEMME exits. CHARLIE-SMITH kisses CLARICE. She lingers in his arms.

CHARLIE-SMITH: I give you all these years.

CLARICE: You must understand.

CHARLIE-SMITH: No. You must understand. Sage-femme says you my heart and our secret be revealed.

CLARICE: Revealed?

CHARLIE-SMITH: To the world when we leave here.

CLARICE: But my life, in New Orleans - -

CHARLIE-SMITH: With me, you always beautiful. You always young. I do anything for you.

CLARICE breaks their embrace. PAUSE as she considers.

CLARICE: Anything?

CHARLIE-SMITH nods. CLARICE considers.

CLARICE: You would.

CHARLIE-SMITH nods.

CLARICE: Yes. You could give me exactly what I need. (beat) You are the best man, Charlie-Smith. I count on you.

CHARLIE-SMITH: Ask it.

CLARICE: Go home. I will call on you and if, if you love me, you will do as I ask.

CHARLIE-SMITH: You know I love you.

CHARLIE-SMITH kisses CLARICE. SAGE-FEMME enters carrying another large mug of tea.

CLARICE: I know. I know very well.

SAGE-FEMME: What you knows?

CHARLIE-SMITH: She knows - -

CLARICE: Charlie-Smith I will see you at the house. Please, go now.

SAGE-FEMME: (to Charlie-Smith) Be safe. Remember.

CHARLIE-SMITH exits.

SAGE-FEMME: What you want here?

CLARICE: I need you to make something for me.

SAGE-FEMME: You already got my best lotion of basil mash and honey to keep those wrinkles away. What else you need?

CLARICE: You told me once that you could be making a strong kind of sleeping tea. You said I be needing to be safe not to be taking too much.

SAGE-FEMME: *Oui.* Why you want that now?

CLARICE: I be wantin' some peaceful sleep to figurin' out - -

SAGE-FEMME: Figure out what?

CLARICE: My life.

SAGE-FEMME: Only yours?

CLARICE: Please. Gimme the tea?

SAGE-FEMME holds out mug.

SAGE-FEMME: Drink.

CLARICE: Not now.

SAGE-FEMME: This not sleeping tea. Belladonna be the sleeping tea. This the reading tea for to see your destiny. Drink.

CLARICE sips reluctantly.

SAGE-FEMME: *Tout.* All of it.

CLARICE gulps down the last of it. SAGE-FEMME takes the mug, holds it in front of CLARICE.

SAGE-FEMME: Spit.

CLARICE: Sage-femme - -

SAGE-FEMME: Spit!

CLARICE spits in the mug. SAGE-FEMME turns the mug, looks at it.

SAGE-FEMME: You jealous of someone, no? You no need to answer, the hawk tells me so. His talons hold a knife. This jealousy will break...a love.

CLARICE: That can't be true.

SAGE-FEMME: The lock. You have obstacles.

CLARICE: I can't be lettin' no obstacles be standin' in my way.

SAGE-FEMME: Funny how you talk so common when you upset. (beat) I keep your secrets for long times.

CLARICE: I never wanted those secrets. I was very young. If Charlie-Smith and I hadn't been dancing in Congo Square that night we would have never - -

SAGE-FEMME: Laid together and created that child you needed to destroy. Had me slice from your body and destroy.

CLARICE: *I* was a child. Set to be with Lucien. It wasn't supposed to happen that way.

SAGE-FEMME: But it did.

CLARICE: We set this in motion sixteen years ago.

SAGE-FEMME: We?

CLARICE: Now I have to fix it, don't you see?

SAGE-FEMME: More secrets you 'spect me to keep?

CLARICE: I take care of you.

SAGE-FEMME: You think I keep that money? I give it to Dove.

CLARICE: To Dove?

SAGE-FEMME: Come all the way to the bayou she does from your big Rue Rampart house. She not too good to spend time with me. We go dance in the square.

CLARICE: Juliet shouldn't be dancing there.

SAGE-FEMME: She no ask for nothing. So I give her the money and tell her to keep it for me. One day, it all gonna be hers so she can buy her own shop.

CLARICE: Please give me the tea. You have to help me.

CLARICE grasps SAGE-FEMME'S hand, mug drops, breaks into a few large pieces.

SAGE-FEMME: I give you nothing. You leave now. Leave.

An African drum beat is heard, soft at first then rising.

CLARICE: All my life I have tried to do what is best for everyone. For Lucien. For Juliet.

SAGE-FEMME: For Ellie? Charlie-Smith?

CLARICE: The best I could. I didn't send them to Georgia.

SAGE-FEMME: They still be slaves.

CLARICE: My life with Lucien cannot change. I have to break any obstacles.

SAGE-FEMME: I leave you to your own destiny.

SAGE-FEMME turns her back on CLARICE and lights a cigar.

CLARICE: Destiny? Juliet cannot have my life. And I will take my secrets to my grave. I will never give up on what I want.

CLARICE secretly grabs the bottle marked belladonna from the shelf, and flees. SAGE-FEMME sings to the beat of the drum.

SAGE-FEMME: (sings)

> Womens lie
> With men forlorn,
> Hearts and bodies
> Lay tattered torn.

Lights and drums fade.

END OF ACT I

ACT II

ACT II, Scene 1

TIME: January 9, 1841. Noon. The day of the Quadroon Ball.

ELLIE is set on the roof in low-light. She is hammering wood into the broken window opening. Amber glow of low candle light illuminates the ornate bed on the landing. CLARICE and CHARLIE-SMITH lie in the bed. He holds her tenderly.

CHARLIE-SMITH: This where I always want to be.

CLARICE: In my big bed.

CHARLIE-SMITH: Here. The attic. On a riverboat. Anywhere with you. You different when it just be the two of us, always has been. Since you was a teenage girl.

CLARICE: A lot has changed since then.

CHARLIE-SMITH: Not everything. There a kindness to you that I don't see when Mister Lucien around.

CLARICE: I wish I had your courage.

CHARLIE-SMITH: I strong for us both when we leave soon.

CLARICE: Do you remember at Sage-femme's this morning when I said you would do something for me?

CHARLIE-SMITH nods.

CLARICE: My heart is heavy with sadness I cannot erase without your help. My home, our home, must be released of this sadness.

CHARLIE-SMITH: What you need me to be doin'?

CLARICE: You will go west - -

CHARLIE-SMITH: We will.

CLARICE: Not right away. I need you to go without me. I will free you.

CHARLIE-SMITH: You say only Mister Lucien has powers to be freein' me.

CLARICE: Trust me. You will have papers to travel and you will go on ahead of me.

CHARLIE-SMITH: You *will* follow?

CLARICE: Yes.

CHARLIE-SMITH: If we go together, right now, we be happy. Why I goin' alone first?

CLARICE: You will not be alone. I will make travel plans for you…with Juliet and Ellie.

CHARLIE-SMITH: You want me to take Dove and Ellie away? Why?

CLARICE: I want Juliet to have the best life she can. And Ellie will take care of her. She loves her.

CHARLIE-SMITH: They both love you.

CLARICE: You said you would do anything for me. Do this.

CHARLIE-SMITH: You askin' too much.

CLARICE rises, wrapping herself in a dressing gown.

CLARICE: Then you do not love me.

CHARLIE-SMITH: Do you love me?

CLARICE: I have cared for you all these years. I give you the best room in the slave quarters. I do not allow Mister Lucien to send you to his cotton fields. I let you tend your horses. And I am with you when and how I can. I give you everything.

CHARLIE-SMITH: You free me? No. And that all I want. *Freedom.* And *you.* Now you lie to Mister Lucien. You lie to Ellie and Dove. You be lyin' to me, too?

CLARICE: No. No. I will never lie to you. You are too smart for that. I am doing this for all for us.

CHARLIE-SMITH: Does Mister Lucien know you plans?

CLARICE: He has no meaning in this.

CHARLIE-SMITH rises from bed.

CHARLIE-SMITH: I think he be the center.

CLARICE: You are my center. I will arrange everything for us to be happy. You three will leave with a wagon and you can take Beacon to pull it.

CHARLIE-SMITH: Beacon? You want me to be takin' Beacon.

CLARICE: Take Beacon or Sunny or whichever horse you want. What does it matter? I will follow in a few days after I am sure Lucien will not pursue us.

CHARLIE-SMITH: You come with me when I leave. You and me. No one else. This be our last chance to escape together.

CLARICE: That will not happen.

CHARLIE-SMITH: You bein' false. I not fallin' into your trap. I be free my own way.

CLARICE: Your way will get you killed.

CHARLIE-SMITH: Your way get me lonely, get me through with you.

CLARICE: You can never be through with me. You belong to me. I own you!

CHARLIE-SMITH: That what you really feel? You own me?

CLARICE: No. No. I love you. You are my strength.

CHARLIE-SMITH: I be *my* strength. With Sage-femme's help.

CLARICE: Do not listen to her! I need you.

CHARLIE-SMITH: You need me in your bed because you own me.

CLARICE: I did not mean it. I was angry. Please, Charlie-Smith, you are my guiding light to happiness.

CHARLIE-SMITH: I need to think.

CLARICE: I do not have time for you to think. You must take them…you must leave today.

CHARLIE-SMITH: I be leavin' soon, Clarice, just not sure who be with me. I need to listen with my heart.

CLARICE: I am your heart!

CHARLIE-SMITH: You were. Are you still?

CHARLIE-SMITH turns, exits. CLARICE gets the bottle of bel-ladonna, hugs it to her. The lights come up on the roof where

181

ELLIE has finished hammering the wood. ELLIE crosses to open the door, it doesn't budge.

ELLIE: (yelling) Someone there? *Ouvrez.* Hello.

CLARICE listens.

ELLIE: (yelling) Someone let me in!

CLARICE starts to exit off the landing, turns, then ascends to the roof.

ELLIE: Let me - -

CLARICE opens the door.

CLARICE: What are you doing?

ELLIE: The door handle stick again when I's hammerin' that wood into the hole. You want to tell me how that old divan flies into that window?

CLARICE: Maybe Juliet was playing in the attic.

ELLIE: Juliet prefer the roof. Maybe you and Charlie-Smith was playin' in the attic.

CLARICE: You forget your place, Ellie.

ELLIE: I remember my place very well.

ELLIE sweeps past CLARICE and descends to the landing.

ELLIE: You best be fixin' that door. It dangerous.

CLARICE: You have no need to go out there again until spring cleaning. I will not bother Lucien with such trivialities when we are getting ready for the ball.

ELLIE: You'd'a bother him if you was stuck out there. Why you in your bedclothes middle of day?

CLARICE: I told you. Getting ready for the ball.

ELLIE: Mmm-hmm. You and Charlie-Smith gettin' brave or stupid.

CLARICE: There is no me and Charlie-Smith anymore. He is just another nigger. Just like you.

ELLIE: And you, lest you be forgettin' that fact.

CLARICE: We are different.

ELLIE: Yes. We are. If you want nothin' goin' on between you and Charlie-Smith, send him up on that roof for awhile in this cold and you'll never have to worry about nothin'.

ELLIE exits to the bedrooms. CLARICE looks towards the roof.

Lights fade.

ACT II, Scene 2

January 9, 1841. Early Afternoon.

Amber glow of low candle light illuminates far downstage left. The rest of the stage is dark. SAGE-FEMME, humming, mixes teas. JULIET, wrapped in cloak, runs onto stage.

SAGE-FEMME: I's been expectin' you.

JULIET: How do you always know?

JULIET hugs SAGE-FEMME.

JULIET: I am so happy.

SAGE-FEMME: I sees that, *ma bébé.*

JULIET: Of course you see. You see everything.

JULIET kisses SAGE-FEMME on the cheek and releases her.

SAGE-FEMME: You be wantin' somethin' of old Sage-femme, *oui?*

JULIET: Since when do I visit and ask for anything?

SAGE-FEMME: Never before. But this be different, no?

JULIET: This *is* different. *I* am different. So much is changing. I just…I want to be sure I'm doing the right thing for everyone.

SAGE-FEMME: Mmm. Drink the tea.

JULIET takes the cup and slowly sips.

JULIET: Sage-femme, the most amazing things are about to happen.

SAGE-FEMME: You be gettin' more than a sewin' shop?

JULIET: Oh yes! A new year. A new life. I'll go to Paris. I'll have love. Protection. My own house!

SAGE-FEMME: Slaves.

JULIET: No. I won't allow that.

SAGE-FEMME: Not up to you.

JULIET: Everything will be up to me. You'll see. And you can come live with me. I'll have rooms for you.

SAGE-FEMME: Why I want to leave my home?

JULIET: I can take care of you. Just like you took care of me when I was little.

SAGE-FEMME: I's fine and happy right were I be. Here, take the money.

SAGE-FEMME gives JULIET a small money roll.

JULIET: I'll keep it in my new house for whenever you want it.

SAGE-FEMME: We see what the leaves say.

SAGE-FEMME pushes the cup to JULIET'S lips. She drinks.

SAGE-FEMME: *Ma bébé,* what you want to know?

JULIET: I don't know. I want to know everything. Or maybe nothing. I wasn't sure I should even ask.

SAGE-FEMME: *Pourquoi?*

JULIET: Isn't it better not knowing? Just living.

SAGE-FEMME: Maybe.

JULIET: Maybe.

SAGE-FEMME: You here now, drink my tea.

JULIET: I want to be sure that everything I've done will work out.

SAGE-FEMME: For who?

JULIET: For me. And, well, for everyone.

SAGE-FEMME: I can not tell you 'bout others. They need to drink for themselves to see what the leaves say.

JULIET: Aunt Clarice is unhappy that I'm...that things are changing. I'm growing up. She doesn't know how to handle all this change. But she has always wanted the best for me.

SAGE-FEMME: Mmm. You be careful.

JULIET: I'm always careful.

SAGE-FEMME: You say yourself, things changin'. Give me the cup.

JULIET: Maybe I shouldn't. If it said anything bad I wouldn't know what to do.

SAGE-FEMME: The leaves guide you. I just read what destiny already written.

JULIET holds tight to the cup.

SAGE-FEMME: You need protectin'.

JULIET: I can protect myself.

SAGE-FEMME: Might be wrong.

JULIET: No. I just had a moment of…question because it is all too good to be true. But I'm fine, really. Everything is perfect. I feel like dancing!

SAGE-FEMME: Give me the cup.

JULIET: I changed my mind. It's better not asking questions, isn't it?

An African drum beat is heard, soft at first then rising. JULIET looks from SAGE-FEMME to the cup. She opens her hands, the cup falls and breaks.

JULIET: Oops. I'll buy you a new one and bring it by sometime tomorrow. Tonight, I'm off to the ball. Cinderella!

JULIET hugs and kisses SAGE-FEMME then exits. SAGE-FEMME bends over the broken cup. She shakes her head, hands to mouth, straightens-up and sings.

SAGE-FEMME:

> You best be watchin'
> Take care, no scorn
> Cuz shrouded bonds
> Bring much to mourn.

Lights fade. Drumbeat intensifies

ACT II, Scene 3

January 9, 1841. Late Afternoon.

LIGHT UP cast by circle of Flambeaux. A masked female African drummer enters, beating loudly. SHE dances, snaking between the Flambeaux. SHE is joined by a second masked female African drummer. They dance around each other. JULIET enters, wrapped in cloak. SHE starts to dance slowly to the beat, then increases her tempo. ELLIE enters.

ELLIE: Dove. I been looking all over for you.

JULIET: You found me.

ELLIE: What you be doin' here. The ball starting in just a few hours. You need to get ready.

JULIET: Dance with me Ellie.

ELLIE: *Ma bébé,* we can't be dancing. We got to get you home.

JULIET: Get ready for my new life. I want one more night to dance in Congo Square.

ELLIE: You can dance after tonight.

JULIET: I'm to be a *placée.*

    JULIET throws off cloak, spins away from ELLIE.

ELLIE: But you be a shop owner one day.

JULIET: Not anymore. I'm going to be loved. I will travel the world.

ELLIE: And have children?

JULIET: Eventually. I suppose. But not right away. I want to live! I'm to be a *placéeeeeeeeeeeee.*

ELLIE: And never a slave.

JULIET: Don't be silly. Of course not. How could a *placée* ever be a slave?

ELLIE: She can't. Ever.

JULIET: Aunt Clarice never dances in Congo Square.

ELLIE: She free. She no need to be dancing here.

JULIET: I'm free too. And I love dancing here. Can I dance here ever after tonight?

ELLIE: I bring you anyplace you want, *ma bébé.*

JULIET: Its all working. I'm so happy.

ELLIE: Is you really?

JULIET: Yes!

ELLIE: I only ever want you to be happy. All my life for that.

JULIET: I'll be happy if you dance with me.

ELLIE: You all grown up now.

JULIET: You think so, too?

> *JULIET spins to ELLIE, ELLIE grabs her hands, pulls JULIET to her, stopping dancing but the drums and masked drummers continue to weave around THEM.*

ELLIE: Look at you. *La fille plus belle dans le monde.*

JULIET: I'm not the most beautiful girl in the world. But I think, tonight, I'm the happiest.

ELLIE: Juliet. Dove. *Je t'aime.*

JULIET: I love you too, Ellie.

ELLIE: You have the life Ellie could never have.

> *ELLIE touches JULIET'S face.*

JULIET: Ellie? What is it?

ELLIE: *Que?* What?

JULIET: You look so serious. Are you alright?

ELLIE: I be happy for you, *ma bébé.* So happy.

JULIET: Well then don't look so glum. Tonight I'll have everything I ever wanted.

ELLIE: And everything I ever wanted for you.

JULIET: Dance with me.

> *JULIET grabs ELLIE'S hands. THEY dance, wildly with abandon, around the Flambeaux with the masked drummers. The drums begin to slow as the dancing slows. The LIGHTS & drums*

FADE as the women come together in a circle. The faint sounds of a grand ball, with people and music, rise.

ACT II, Scene 4

TIME: *January 9, 1841. Evening.*

LIGHTS UP on the Grand Ballroom of the Quadroon Ball. Faint sounds of ball music and people continue. LUCIEN enters dressed in finery, a decorated riding crop slid into one belt holster and a small pistol in the other. He struts around like the master of his world. He inspects the setting, pours a brandy, unholsters his gun and inspects it. CHARLIE-SMITH, dressed in a simple suit, enters.

CHARLIE-SMITH: Mister Lucien.

LUCIEN: Look at this pistol, Charlie-Smith. She's a beauty but getting outdated. Only one shot. A single shot is not in style anymore. I ordered one of Colt's new multi-chamber revolvers. Had hoped to have it for the holidays, show it off a bit, but it hasn't arrived yet. Such longing, always the way when something new comes along.

CHARLIE-SMITH: Yes, Mister Lucien.

LUCIEN holsters his pistol.

LUCIEN: The horses are secured with the others?

CHARLIE-SMITH: Yes, Sir.

LUCIEN: Good. You can go to Congo Square for a few hours, if you like.

CHARLIE-SMITH: Mister Lucien, I be hoping to talk with you.

LUCIEN: About the ball?

CHARLIE-SMITH: No, Sir.

LUCIEN: Then it can wait.

CHARLIE-SMITH: No, Sir.

LUCIEN: *Pardon?*

CHARLIE-SMITH: Mister Lucien, I serve you well all my life.

LUCIEN: Best blacksmith around. Clarice loves you //

CHARLIE-SMITH: Sir?

LUCIEN: // taking care of Sunny.

CHARLIE-SMITH: Yes, Sir. But, thing is, I be wanting my chance that Sage-femme and my mama and papa had. Chance to be free.

LUCIEN: This is not the time, Charlie-Smith.

CHARLIE-SMITH: Has to be. Time real important. I be needing to know now, if you give me that. I think I deserve it.

LUCIEN: You think so?

CHARLIE-SMITH: Yes, Sir. And I be promising to leave New Orleans so you don't have to put up no monies for guarantee, Sir.

LUCIEN: Now is not the time.

CHARLIE-SMITH: Be no other time than now.

LUCIEN: Another time is truly required, Charlie-Smith.

CHARLIE-SMITH: No, Sir. I need my answer tonight. I need to be getting my life set.

LUCIEN: Your life is already set.

CHARLIE-SMITH: Sir, I - -

LUCIEN: Enough! (with cold calm) Do you see that I am here to enjoy a lovely evening? You bother me with this now? It is unacceptable. Now or ever. (beat) Charlie-Smith, I am expected to keep a certain lifestyle. To have certain privileges. You are simply part of the whole that is my life. Freedom? You should understand that, in my households, with all that I give you, you are as free as you will ever be. Now, get out of my sight.

CHARLIE-SMITH, enraged, turns towards exit. CLARICE enters. They both stop, look at each other. CHARLIE-SMITH breaks the hold and exits angrily. LUCIEN smiles and crosses to CLARICE.

CLARICE: Is everything alright, Lucien?

LUCIEN: Nothing to worry your pretty little head about, *ma chère*.

CLARICE: Charlie-Smith looked angry

LUCIEN: He wants his freedom. I cannot give it to him.

CLARICE: Did he say anything more?

LUCIEN: About?

CLARICE: Nothing.

LUCIEN: You look lovely.

CLARICE: Thank you.

LUCIEN kisses her, spins her about the room.

LUCIEN: You still make me happy.

CLARICE: But not completely.

LUCIEN: As much as you can, *ma chère*. And I love you for this. Eternally. (beat) Is Dove prepared?

CLARICE: We can still stop this, Lucien.

LUCIEN shakes his head 'no'.

CLARICE: Please.

LUCIEN: You should not be so fearful. Dove will have the best life possible. Paris. Protection. Children.

CLARICE: Children. Are you sure? She seems more intent on travel than children.

LUCIEN: She'll have both. First travel. Then children.

CLARICE: And if she refuses?

LUCIEN: Refuses? She'll do as I say. Just as you do.

CLARICE: She has been groomed for more.

LUCIEN: I do not like too hurt you by saying such things but, as we know, nothing can be more than children.

CLARICE: Please, Lucien. You have no idea what you are setting in motion.

LUCIEN: It is already in motion.

CLARICE: Juliet cannot. She cannot. Be in *plaçage*. With *you*!

PAUSE as LUCIEN smiles.

CLARICE: I see it when you look at her, talk to her, laugh and touch. I know you, Lucien.

LUCIEN: And I you. This is not for you to concern yourself with. Nothing will change between us.

CLARICE: It gives you one more entire household to manage. Your wife, another *placée*. Where does that leave me? Us?

LUCIEN: It leaves you exactly where you have always been. I promise.

CLARICE: But she is only fifteen!

LUCIEN: Sixteen next week. What better birthday gift?

CLARICE: You are forty-five, Lucien! It's perverse!

LUCIEN: I will not be bound by puritanical dictates.

CLARICE: No. Lucien, no!

LUCIEN: You have given me everything, *ma chère*, including the gift of Dove by bringing her to our household.

CLARICE: Not for you to take into *plaçage*!

LUCIEN: I did not plan this but everything about her quickens me. How could I not love her? You love her.

CLARICE: As an aunt. And you should love her as an uncle.

LUCIEN: She is vibrant, audacious, young as you were when I first fell in love with you. Because I love her, does not diminish my love for you.

CLARICE: You're not in love with her.

LUCIEN: You will trust me, trust that even as Dove bears my children my love for you will remain.

CLARICE: It won't.

LUCIEN: I expected you to be happy for me. You know having children is something I long for. Have I loved you any less because you cannot give me them? Never. Felt differently about my wife for the same? No. And I will not love Dove anymore because she can give them to me.

JULIET enters the ballroom, followed by ELLIE. JULIET is dressed as a woman in a stunning gown, abundant decolletage, all-grown-up. ELLIE is in a simple, quiet dress.

LUCIEN: How can you deny me *that*?

JULIET reaches LUCIEN and CLARICE, curtsies.

CLARICE: Your dress.

JULIET: It was delivered by courier this morning.

LUCIEN: I had to guess on the size.

JULIET: It's perfect. Thank you. Lucien.

CLARICE: But she had a dress.

ELLIE: This here one be prettier than that ole plain thing you give her. Prettier even than the one we made.

LUCIEN: Your work is beautiful, as always, Ellie.

ELLIE: Thank you.

The music rises, changes.

CLARICE: Lucien, dance with me?

LUCIEN: (waving off Clarice) The next one. Right now, I think I would like to see how this new dress I bought moves on the dance floor. Dove, may I have this dance?

JULIET looks at CLARICE. LUCIEN takes hold of JULIET'S hand, leads her to center stage. They dance while CLARICE and ELLIE look on.

ELLIE: Dove bein' presented. I joyous.

CLARICE: Joyous? Really? She was set to own a shop. To be truly free from any demands of society.

ELLIE: And now she don't be working for nobody. She be cared for, loved, a woman of property.

CLARICE: All of that comes with a price, Ellie. You know this.

ELLIE: A price you happy to pay.

CLARICE: A price I had to pay. My mother gave me no choice and, yes, I have privilege because of this. Privilege I won't give up. Not for Dove. Not for anyone.

ELLIE: Privilege good enough for you. It good enough for Dove.

CLARICE: Everything would have been fine if she just did as planned.

ELLIE: Child grow up.

CLARICE: Her growing up will not cost me my life. Do you not understand? Lucien wants to take her as *his placée.*

ELLIE: Lucien want Dove as his own?

CLARICE: Look at them.

ELLIE: And he has said he takes her?

CLARICE nods.

CLARICE: I know Lucien. And you are not blind. You have seen it, too. The way he reacts to her. He has asked for her hand in *plaçage* and if I refuse he will put me out.

ELLIE: Then you will not refuse.

CLARICE: We have never spoken openly of what might have been and what is.

ELLIE: What is? I a slave.

CLARICE: Only Lucien can free you.

ELLIE: You could'a asked, swayed him.

CLARICE: You said yourself Lucien controls everyone.

ELLIE: That includes you.

CLARICE: You meant you, too. When we first came to this house together? Is that why you hid your pregnancy from him? Answer me! Who is Juliet's father?

ELLIE: I take that to my grave.

CLARICE: You cannot do that. I need to know the truth!

ELLIE: It no matter who her papa is.

CLARICE: Of course it matters. If it is Lucien he cannot…this cannot happen. I will send you away. Both of you. With money and transport papers. Juliet is free. I will free you.

ELLIE: You just says only Mister Lucien can free me.

CLARICE: I will figure out a way. You will go west. I will send Charlie-Smith to keep you safe. But you all must leave now, immediately after the ball. Before Lucien comes to take Juliet to a new home tomorrow. We can do this. You will all be free.

ELLIE: And then you be free of all of us. Free to be with Mister Lucien without me or Dove or Charlie-Smith.

CLARICE: You are not listening to me. He is her *father*.

ELLIE: It no matter.

CLARICE: How can you say that?

ELLIE: What if all you say is true. Would it be so bad? He will buy her a home. He will provide for her care. He will love her, keep her highest in the status she can achieve for herself. This is the best for her. The *best*.

CLARICE: What kind of mother are you?

ELLIE: The kind that know what be best for her child.

CLARICE: What if she comes with child? What then?

ELLIE: We both know what to do with child to be gone, don't we?

CLARICE: Listen to yourself. You do not know what you are saying!

ELLIE: Know more about it than you do. Lucien will love her. She will be better than me. Better than any shop owner. Better than you. And that's what worry you so stop bein' false.

CLARICE: I will tell him.

ELLIE: You will not.

CLARICE: I will tell him that you are her mother. That she is a slave. That you blackmailed me into this arrangement. I will tell him!

ELLIE: And I will tell him of you and Charlie-Smith. Of a Negro baby sliced out of your womb sixteen years ago and destroyed. Of how you never have Master Lucien's children ever because of the damage done.

CLARICE: I did that for him. For us. For us to be together.

ELLIE: You did that for you. For your life of privilege.

CLARICE: If I could change it…

ELLIE: You change nothing. You still lay with Charlie-Smith. I will tell him. Don't think I won't. Dove will be Lucien's *placée* with all of the privileges. And if a child come, we, you and me, will take her to where we know to go. To Sage-femme. I will never, ever let her be a slave. Ever!

LUCIEN: (to Dove as they dance) You had to be the most beautiful Quadroon here. Look about, my Dove, all the others are jealous.

JULIET: You're making me blush.

ELLIE: Without this, she would only have a shop to work in. Or worse.

CLARICE: If everything had stayed the same, I would not have let anything bad happen to her.

ELLIE: He guarantee it.

LUCIEN: I love it when you blush. I want to make you blush everyday.

JULIET: It is you, isn't it? Who wants me?

CLARICE: He guarantees many things. But the price is high.

LUCIEN laughs.

JULIET: I didn't mean to…if it isn't…I couldn't tell at Antoine's if you were thinking the same thing I was. I don't want to assume.

LUCIEN: I would be honored if you would consider it.

JULIET: I have loved you since I was a little girl.

LUCIEN: I, also, but my love has changed. I feel connected now as protector and *placée*.

LUCIEN & CLARICE: (dual dialog) Everything will be different.

ELLIE: Dove will be happy.

CLARICE: *I* will be happy.

ELLIE: You love him.

CLARICE: He is mine.

ELLIE: Charlie-Smith?

CLARICE: Not anymore.

LUCIEN: I will give you a home more magnificent than any other on *Rue Rampart*. I will see you every weekend.

JULIET: How will you make all this happen? Take care of so many?

ELLIE: Charlie-Smith gonna leave.

CLARICE: I do not care.

ELLIE: You don't forget sixteen years like it nothing.

LUCIEN & CLARICE: (dual dialog) You would be surprised how easy it is.

JULIET: Will you now speak to Aunt Clarice?

LUCIEN: I will.

JULIET: I have a favor to ask you.

LUCIEN: *Oui.*

JULIET: I want to talk to Aunt Clarice before you speak with her, if I may?

LUCIEN: I'm not sure that is wise.

JULIET: Please.

CLARICE: I did my best for you. For her.

ELLIE: You go with life cuz there be no other way. You think I like standing by and not telling Dove I is her mama? You think that easy? No. So you will not stop this. She will never be a slave.

LUCIEN: I think I may say yes to anything for you.

JULIET: Promise?

LUCIEN: (laughs) Perhaps I have bitten off more than I can chew with such a bold young woman.

JULIET: You like me bold.

LUCIEN: (laughs) I do. I have another surprise for my bold Dove.

CLARICE: It isn't done, yet.

ELLIE: It is.

CLARICE: You think so?

LUCIEN: I am going to give you Charlie-Smith and Ellie for your slaves.

JULIET: No. Aunt Clarice will be heartbroken.

LUCIEN: It was her idea, so to speak.

JULIET: They will be mine to do with as I please?

LUCIEN: *Oui.*

JULIET: I will free them.

ELLIE & JULIET: (dual dialog) It will be done.

CLARICE: No, it will not. It. Will. Not.

LUCIEN: Anything to make you smile, Dove. We'll have the best life. Beautiful children.

JULIET: But first, Paris.

LUCIEN: *Oui, bien sûr.* You make me feel young.

JULIET: Eternally.

LUCIEN kisses JULIET deeply. CLARICE makes a move towards them. ELLIE stops her. LUCIEN takes JULIET by the arm, crosses to CLARICE and ELLIE.

LUCIEN: (to Clarice) You will follow tradition tonight.

CLARICE: We have not made an agreement.

LUCIEN: (to Juliet) We *have* made an agreement. Juliet has agreed.

CLARICE: Lucien, you have not thought this through.

LUCIEN: Juliet, your aunt will instruct you on certain customs and traditions of pleasing me. Clarice, Juliet wishes to speak with you alone, first.

ELLIE: I'd like to stay.

LUCIEN: I think not.

LUCIEN glares at ELLIE. They exit.

CLARICE: What do you want?

JULIET: I want everyone to be happy.

CLARICE: He does not love you. You are a prize to be attained. A battle to be won. Young. A challenge.

JULIET: He loves me. He loves you, too.

CLARICE: And his wife and his horses and his mansions and ships and cotton. I will always be first, though.

JULIET: Yes. Of course. Aunt Clarice, I want you to be happy.

CLARICE: I am happy. What makes you think I am not happy?

JULIET: This must be difficult.

CLARICE: You know nothing.

JULIET: I'm only trying to tell you - -

CLARICE: Stop talking like that! The proper pronunciation is I am, not I'm.

JULIET: I *am* going to be good to him.

CLARICE: I already am.

JULIET: We could be like sisters. Helping each other. He will be with me on weekends and his wife during the beginning of the week - -

CLARICE: What did you just say?

JULIET: Sisters. It could be good for us, more important, for him.

CLARICE: About weekends.

JULIET: He has said he will be with me on weekends.

CLARICE: He is with me on weekends. (beat) You are already changing him.

JULIET: If you will only give me a chance. His happiness is our duty.

CLARICE: *Our* duty. And there is another side to the headstrong Juliet.

JULIET: I do not mean to be but he has made his choice and that will not change. Of course, being new to him, young, bold as he likes, maybe I can sway him into splitting that time. If we were sisters.

LUCIEN enters.

CLARICE: Headstrong and sly.

LUCIEN: Who is sly? Certainly not my Dove.

LUCIEN crosses to JULIET, embraces her with one arm. He opens his other arm towards CLARICE. CLARICE does not move.

LUCIEN: Your talk is done?

CLARICE nods. LUCIEN beckons CLARICE with his hands. CLARICE crosses into LUCIEN'S other arm. LUCIEN kisses each woman's head.

LUCIEN: *Bon.* My little girls. I love you both. And Juliet will make me a father. Think of it, a house full of children. I am very happy because of you.

JULIET: We will be happy, Lucien.

LUCIEN looks at CLARICE, waiting for a response. PAUSE. CLARICE does not respond. LUCIEN releases JULIET.

LUCIEN: Dove. Leave us, now.

JULIET: Shouldn't I hear…

LUCIEN gives JULIET an amused stare. JULIET curtsies and exits.

LUCIEN: What did she want?

CLARICE: To tell me you love me.

LUCIEN: You already know that.

CLARICE: So you say.

LUCIEN: Your insecurities are beginning to wear, Clarice. Your temper tantrums will only serve to keep me from your bed, especially now.

CLARICE: You are already planning the exodus from my bed.

LUCIEN: You will be a doting aunt, as you have been, and I will love you even more than I do now. You believe me, don't you?

PAUSE

LUCIEN: Say yes.

PAUSE

LUCIEN: Come now, Clarice. *Oui?*

PAUSE

LUCIEN: I suggest you smile and accept. I would hate for our life together to...*change*...if you do not.

PAUSE

CLARICE: Very well.

LUCIEN: Very well?

CLARICE: I will accept.

LUCIEN: I did not hear a yes.

PAUSE

LUCIEN: Yes?

CLARICE: Yes.

LUCIEN: And your earlier concerns?

CLARICE: My duty is to make you happy.

LUCIEN: Yes. It is.

CLARICE: And you do everything to make me happy.

LUCIEN: I always have.

CLARICE: Of course. You are the master of your world.

LUCIEN: (chuckling) I am the master of much, Clarice, even though it is not always easy.

CLARICE: I only mean to point out that you chose your paths in life. I admire you for that. I have come around to your way of thinking. And, now, I hope you will come around to mine, as a reward for my duty.

LUCIEN: (chuckling) So you are not being completely magnanimous. What bauble would you like? A new horsehair brush for those 100 strokes each night? A new corset to tighten you waist? More potions and lotions of youth, perhaps? What is it, Clarice?

CLARICE: No acquisitions. Simply a transfer of property.

LUCIEN: What property do you have in mind? If you think I am going to sell your home and buy something large enough for me to protect both you and Dove under one roof, that would be, how did you put it...perverse.

CLARICE: I have no such thought.

PAUSE as LUCIEN eyes CLARICE.

CLARICE: I wish you to dispose of some properties which have been disagreeable...will cause problems with your *plaçage* to Juliet.

LUCIEN: You are the only one who would cause problems.

CLARICE: No. I will take her to my home tonight, as is tradition. I will instruct her on the ways of pleasing you. We will bond.

LUCIEN: You are already bound together.

CLARICE: We will bond like...sisters. We will share *beignets* and tea. Enjoy our last night together under one roof before you spirit her away to her new home. (pause) But, there are others who consider you taking Juliet in *plaçage* as damaging to her.

LUCIEN: Who has said this? I will deal with them.

CLARICE: They think you are too old. Too attached to others to truly look out for Juliet's interest.

LUCIEN: Enough with your dancing. Tell me now.

CLARICE: You must sell Ellie and Charlie-Smith.

LUCIEN: Again with disposing of them.

CLARICE: They love Juliet.

LUCIEN: As do I.

CLARICE: But in very different ways.

LUCIEN: They will come around.

CLARICE: I do not want them to come around. I want them gone. I am giving you Juliet.

LUCIEN: You forget yourself.

CLARICE: If you love me then you will do this for me.

LUCIEN: Charlie-Smith is the best blacksmith in the city and Ellie has been with you since you were born. How can you imagine this?

CLARICE: I am only looking out for you, as is my duty.

LUCIEN: I am not sure I believe you. (beat) Charlie-Smith and Ellie are quite popular this evening. But...perhaps.

CLARICE: You will do this for me?

LUCIEN: Arrangements might be made.

CLARICE: Send them to your friend in Georgia.

LUCIEN: He would not treat them kindly.

CLARICE: I do not care. I want them gone so they can never defy me again.

LUCIEN: I thought this was about me. (beat) Very well, I will send them away.

CLARICE: Lucien. Thank you!

LUCIEN: They will go to Dove's home.

CLARICE: What? No!

LUCIEN: This evening both you and Juliet have tried to coax me into doing something with Charlie-Smith and Ellie.

CLARICE: But she wants you to free them.

LUCIEN: She has such faith in this world. Perhaps she can quicken that in me, again.

CLARICE: That will cost you thousands of dollars. I want them gone. As slaves. Far, far away.

LUCIEN: Juliet will get them as a gift, to do with as she pleases. I will find others, pulled from the field, which should make them happy, to serve in your household. And you? You will do as tradition beholds tonight. With *beignets* and tea. How sweet.

CLARICE: No, Lucien. They must be gone. Far away. Charlie-Smith is going to...is going...

LUCIEN: Charlie-Smith is going to continue to serve my horses and my households. End of story.

CLARICE: They are planning an uprising.

LUCIEN: Who?

CLARICE: Charlie-Smith and others.

LUCIEN: A lie to make me do as you wish?

CLARICE: The slaves plan to fight.

LUCIEN: If what you say is true, they will be thwarted just as others have been. This is not Virginia. They have no Nat Turner. And we are Native Creoles. We will suppress them. If I were you, I would be more concerned about what I will find out when I dig into the real reasons you want Charlie-Smith and Ellie gone.

LUCIEN kisses CLARICE.

LUCIEN: You keep me on my toes. You will always be my clever girl, and Juliet will be my...saving grace.

LUCIEN dances CLARICE around the room. Suddenly gunfire is heard. JULIET runs into the ballroom.

JULIET: They're shooting at us.

LUCIEN rushes to JULIET.

LUCIEN: No one will hurt you.

JULIET: They're in the courtyard. They'll be up here soon.

LUCIEN: Where is Ellie? Why is she not with you?

JULIET: She ran towards them. Who would do this?

CLARICE: Charlie-Smith.

LUCIEN: They will be stopped.

BEAT as LUCIEN unholsters his gun. JULIET clings to him.

LUCIEN: Clarice, take Juliet home. Get to safety. Hide if you must.

CLARICE stands shock still.

Clarice. Listen to me!

Gunfire and shouting are heard.

Clarice, do as you are told!

CHARLIE-SMITH bursts onto the stage, gun in hand. LUCIEN pushes JULIET out of the way as he and CHARLIE-SMITH draw on each other. CLARICE steps between them. CHARLIE-SMITH looks at the three of them, runs across the stage, and exits. LUCIEN looks at CLARICE. Lights fade.

ACT II, Scene 5

TIME: January 9, 1841. Late evening.

The sound of turmoil is heard: people shouting, gunfire. Low-light of the bayou illuminates down stage left as SAGE-FEMME enters carrying a lantern. ELLIE follows behind her.

ELLIE: Comes to the house. It be safer there.

SAGE-FEMME: No one gonna bother a old woman like me.

ELLIE: This an uprising. The white men see your skin, they don't care who you are, they just shoot.

SAGE-FEMME: They no see me. It so cold I all bundled up, just like you.

ELLIE: You can't hide your face!

SAGE-FEMME: I seen this coming. The leaves show destiny.

ELLIE: Not my destiny.

CHARLIE-SMITH runs on-stage carrying his gun.

SAGE-FEMME: His.

CHARLIE-SMITH: They shooting to kill. We do the same.

ELLIE: Charlie-Smith, come back to the house. We hide there.

CHARLIE-SMITH: You think I go back there? I free. Come with me, Ellie. I got a boat, go upriver. Got a compass, too.

ELLIE: Compass?

CHARLIE-SMITH takes out LUCIEN'S mother-of-pearl compass.

CHARLIE-SMITH: Clarice bought this compass for *him* but now it be *mine*. And it point north. To Illinois. Then point west.

SAGE-FEMME: You make your choice.

SAGE-FEMME enters her shack. ELLIE and CHARLIE-SMITH follow.

CHARLIE-SMITH: Clarice made it for me. I coulda ended it. Shot him right through. She coulda left with me but she step between us. She save him.

SAGE-FEMME: To kill you. Then you should know she meant to send you both to Georgia.

SAGE-FEMME holds up a large shard from the cup CLARICE broke earlier.

208

ELLIE: Georgia?

SAGE-FEMME: Her secrets would go with you.

CHARLIE-SMITH: All her secrets.

SAGE-FEMME: You take care of *you* Charlie-Smith.

CHARLIE-SMITH: We gonna fight our way to freedom.

SAGE-FEMME: You can not win this fight. They has more weapons.

CHARLIE-SMITH: We have more hate.

SAGE-FEMME: You leave that hate with this city.

CHARLIE-SMITH: I gonna make it, Sage-femme. Ellie?

ELLIE: I not leave.

CHARLIE-SMITH: Nothing here for you.

SAGE-FEMME: She never leave Dove. Dove be home.

CHARLIE-SMITH: Not my home. Not no more.

ELLIE: Be safe, Charlie-Smith.

SAGE-FEMME: Hide during the day. Travel at night. And if you get caught, if they send you to the fields, or to the gallows, I got something for to send you to the promised land, your own way.

SAGE-FEMME searches for the belladonna on her shelf.

CHARLIE-SMITH: What it be?

SAGE-FEMME: Belladonna. You drink lots, close your eyes, wake in the promised land. (beat) But it gone. (beat) Clarice.

ELLIE: What 'bout her?

SAGE-FEMME: She told me she wanted it for sleep. For peace. But now I think she means to bring harm with it.

209

CHARLIE-SMITH: Bring harm? To herself? Tell me. You read the leaves. Did she mean harm herself?

SAGE-FEMME: No matter now. You through with her.

CHARLIE-SMITH: It matters!

SAGE-FEMME: (to Ellie) You best be getting back to Dove, quick as you can.

ELLIE: Nothing gonna happen to her. Mister Lucien makes sure of that.

SAGE-FEMME: This not his say. This destiny.

> ELLIE *runs off-stage.* SAGE-FEMME *looks at* CHARLIE-SMITH *who looks at his gun. Lights fade.*

ACT II, Scene 6

TIME: January 9, 1841. Midnight.

LIGHTS UP on the drawing room. JULIET is pacing. CLARICE is looking into the courtyard. The sound of turmoil continues: people shouting, gunfire.

JULIET: I'm frightened.

CLARICE: Lucien will take care of everything.

JULIET: How can you be so calm?

CLARICE: I know what he is capable of. He will suppress this rebellion just like three years ago.

JULIET: People are dying.

CLARICE: People *are* dying.

JULIET: I just said - -

CLARICE: Many people. Are dying.

JULIET: What?

CLARICE: Death.

JULIET: What are you - -

CLARICE: I will fix us some tea.

JULIET: How can you think of tea at a time like this?

CLARICE crosses to courtyard exit. JULIET rushes to her.

JULIET: Where are you going?

CLARICE: Kitchen.

JULIET: Did you check the rest of the house? What if someone has broken in?

CLARICE: I checked. We are safe. For now.

JULIET: For now?

CLARICE: Tea, Juliet.

CLARICE begins to exit.

JULIET: Don't leave me.

CLARICE: Not to worry. I am just going to the kitchen.

JULIET: Outside?

CLARICE: It *is* through the courtyard.

JULIET: You can't go outside. What if someone is out there? You could be hurt. Please don't go.

JULIET grabs on to CLARICE.

JULIET: I don't want any tea! I want to be safe. We should be hiding as Lucien said.

CLARICE removes herself from JULIET'S grasp.

CLARICE: Tea would calm us both.

JULIET: You can't leave.

CLARICE: A drink then. Champagne? No. Brandy. Brandy will calm us. Trust me.

CLARICE guides JULIET to the settee, crosses to bar, pours a glass of brandy. She takes the bottle of belladonna from her pocket, looks at it thoughtfully, puts it back in her pocket. She crosses back to JULIET with the drink.

CLARICE: Here. Drink up.

JULIET: I've never had - -

CLARICE: Now is not the time for decorum.

CLARICE pushes the glass to JULIET'S lips. JULIET sips and spits it out, coughing.

JULIET: I don't want anymore.

CLARICE: It will calm us.

CLARICE nods, coaxing JULIET.

JULIET: Thank you for being a good aunt. And I know we'll be good sisters. Taking care of Lucien together. He'll love us both and you'll love our children.

JULIET reaches for the glass of brandy. CLARICE pulls it away, crosses to bar.

JULIET: Was that enough?

CLARICE pours all belladonna into JULIET'S glass, returns glass to JULIET.

CLARICE: There is no other way.

JULIET tries to sip. CLARICE tips glass. JULIET chokes and gulps at the same time, drinking half the glass.

CLARICE: I'm sorry, Juliet.

JULIET: Sorry?

CLARICE touches JULIET'S hair and face.

CLARICE: Do you feel better?

JULIET shakes her head 'no'.

CLARICE: You will. Soon. It will be just like sleeping.

JULIET: We should hide in our rooms.

CLARICE tips glass. JULIET finishes the brandy, coughing.

CLARICE: Just a matter of time now.

JULIET: I don't want to wait.

CLARICE: Soon.

JULIET: Now! I'm scared. Please. Hide.

CLARICE: Perhaps you are right. Somewhere no one would find us. We can go to Sage-femme's. Through the bayou. Plenty of places to hide there.

JULIET: We can't leave the house.

CLARICE: *My* house.

JULIET: There has to be a safe place here. Under our beds? In the armoires?

CLARICE pulls JULIET to her feet.

I'm not leaving!

JULIET pulls away.

(less frantic) We'll lock the doors. There has to be…I have to think of someplace. No. Yes. The attic.

CLARICE: Alright. We'll hide here. Someplace safe where no one will find you. Because if they find us, they might not just kill us, Juliet. They could do worse. They could defile us and then Lucien would not want you.

JULIET: (sluggish) Lucien will…

JULIET swoons, slumps onto the settee.

CLARICE: Will what? Juliet?

JULIET: Find…protect.

CLARICE: I must protect what is mine. Surely you understand.

JULIET: I am…Cinderella. Don't feel right.

CLARICE: You are scared. I will get you to safety. (beat) The roof. You love the roof. A perfect place to hide in your perch. Dove.

JULIET: (sleepy) Freezing.

CLARICE helps JULIET to her feet. JULIET is a wobbly, shuffles her feet.

JULIET: Too cold…out…side.

CLARICE guides JULIET up the stairs.

CLARICE: It will only be for a short time. Sleep. Dear. Child.

JULIET: You…hide. I don't want harm to you.

CLARICE: You won't feel a thing. I promise.

JULIET: Coat.

CLARICE: I will get it. Not a moment to lose. Hurry.

CLARICE opens roof door, guides JULIET out. CLARICE closes roof door.

PAUSE as JULIET leans against door, grasps handle with both hands, tries to turn it - it does not budge. CLARICE pauses before descending to landing. JULIET tries again, without success, to open the door.

JULIET: Love…you.

CLARICE descends to drawing room. JULIET does not move, slumped against the door, hands on the door handle. CLARICE looks at herself in the mirror. The noises of turmoil get louder. LUCIEN rushes in.

LUCIEN: Did that nigger Charlie-Smith show up here?

CLARICE: No.

LUCIEN: Draw a gun on me. I will kill him. If he's not already dead.

CLARICE: Dead?

LUCIEN: I promise you that.

LUCIEN crosses to bar, sets down gun, pours & drinks. Looks around.

LUCIEN: Where is Juliet? She is safe, *oui*?

CLARICE looks towards the roof. JULIET slides to the floor, hands still on the handle. She tries to open door, it does not open.

LUCIEN: I asked you a question? Is. She. Safe?

CLARICE: I lost her in the crowd.

LUCIEN: You what?

CLARICE: It was chaos. Gunfire. Shouting. We ran. Scared. We got to Congo Square. There were so many people. I held her tight but someone fired at us. We ducked and lost our grip. I tried to find her. She just disappeared.

LUCIEN: Do not worry. I will find her.

CLARICE touches LUCIEN'S face. CHARLIE-SMITH enters.

CHARLIE-SMITH: (to Clarice) You're alive.

LUCIEN: You won't be for long.

CHARLIE-SMITH quickly draws his gun on LUCIEN.

CHARLIE-SMITH: You tried to send me to Georgia? Meant to kill me?

LUCIEN: This is the second time tonight you dare to draw a gun on me. I *will* kill you.

CHARLIE-SMITH: Clarice, all these years. Sixteen years in your bed. Do you think I don't know about our baby and what you done?

LUCIEN looks at CLARICE.

LUCIEN: Clarice?

CLARICE: Liar! You're trying to escape and you want us all to pay. Lucien, you can't believe him.

LUCIEN: (to Clarice) You stepped between us at the ball. Who were you trying to protect?

CLARICE: You! Only you!

LUCIEN: Or only you?

CLARICE: He lies!

As CHARLIE-SMITH and CLARICE glare at each other, LUCIEN slowly makes his way to his gun.

CHARLIE-SMITH: That all we was, a lie. All of it. You never love me.

CLARICE: You're a slave!

CHARLIE-SMITH: You a slave, too! Free woman of color? Ain't no such thing in *plaçage*. And you know it!

CLARICE: I hate you!

An African drum beat is heard, soft at first. LUCIEN reaches his gun, grabs at it, spins and fires. He misses. ELLIE enters just as CHARLIE-SMITH fires at LUCIEN with a direct hit. LUCIEN stumbles towards the stairs, CLARICE follows him.

CLARICE: Lucien!

LUCIEN falls onto the lower stairs. On the roof, one of JULIET'S hands slips from the door handle.

ELLIE: (to Charlie-Smith) Go before they hang you.

CHARLIE-SMITH: It all a lie.

ELLIE: Please.

CHARLIE-SMITH: Freedom, Ellie. I free of it all.

CHARLIE-SMITH exits. ELLIE crosses to CLARICE who holds the dead LUCIEN.

ELLIE: Where be Dove?

CLARICE: Lucien. You *can't* be dead.

ELLIE: Clarice. Where be Dove?

CLARICE: What'll I do?

ELLIE tries to pull CLARICE off of LUCIEN, to shake her.

No!

CLARICE grabs LUCIEN'S gun and points it at ELLIE. ELLIE backs away.

Leave us alone! This is all your fault. All of it.

CLARICE pulls the trigger, shaking the gun, no bullet emerges. She throws the gun away.

ELLIE: Tell me where she be.

CLARICE is unresponsive. ELLIE looks into courtyard, under stairs, about the room. She then, slowly, ascends stairs. ELLIE gets to the landing, looks down towards the bedrooms.

Where my *bébé* be?

ELLIE looks towards the roof. JULIET'S other hand finally slips from the door handle. PAUSE as JULIET is completely, utter-

ly, dead still. ELLIE slowly rises, opens the roof door, rushes to JULIET. DRUMBEAT gets louder.

Lights fade on stage except for a faint glow around CLARICE and LUCIEN and around ELLIE and JULIET.

SAGE-FEMME enters with her lantern. She sings.

SAGE-FEMME: (sings)

> Deep in the bayou
> When child is born,
> And secrets silence
> The pact. Is. Sworn.

Lights and drumbeat fade.

END OF PLAY

Lagniappe

I LIKE

CHARACTER

MAGGIE: Age 13. Torn between many disparate worlds, between youth and growing up, between love and loss, between boys and girls.

TIME

Present day. Early Carnival season: day after Krewe de Vieux parade.

SETTING

The fountain of a Garden District mansion in New Orleans.

SETTING NOTE

Stage edge could be used for the setting.

PRONUNCIATION

Krewe = crew. Vieux = view.

During the monologue MAGGIE is seated in the edge of the fountain, feet in the water as she pulls apart plastic Mardi Gras beads, tossing beads into the fountain.

MAGGIE: Last night, I snuck off to the Krewe du Vieux parade in the Quarter. I've never done *anything* like that before.

Don't tell my moms.

They'd go all Transformers on me. Especially because Vieux had a guy dressed as a giant...well, as a huge...you know...a boy's...penis. And they think I've never seen one.

I have, ya know. Snuck a peek in the boys' locker room once.

They're kinda gross.

PAUSE

I went to the parade with a boy. Don't tell my moms! I mean they're all sensitive to me about it.

"You can like boys or girls, Maggie-Mae."

I know that!

But they won't let me date until I'm sixteen. Sixteen! Juliet was thirteen, my age, when she fell in love with Romeo.

PAUSE

Okay, that didn't end well. Bad example. But there have to be others.

So I think I like...boys. Some boys are cute, right? Austin Mahone. Elyar Fox.

Although Jennifer Lawrence is cute. And don't even get me started on Selena Gomez.

PAUSE

But, lately, I've seen how really...mean girls can be.

They yell so loud sometimes I think my bedroom windows are gonna break. I don't think I heard the word "bitch" as much in my whole life as I have the last few months.

That's why I snuck out last night. I had to get away from their fighting.

PAUSE

I tried to be good, to make them see I'd be good if they'd stay together.

But they told me yesterday. And gave me the whole "its not your fault and we both love you" speech.

So, yeah, I'm gonna like...boys.

Even if I like girls. Girls are mean.

Don't tell my moms.

MAGGIE kicks the water with her feet, tosses the last beads into the fountain as light fade.

END OF PLAY

TOMATO

CAST

SAMMIE: Mid-20s to 30s. Wearing crumpled clothing that she could have taken from the dirty laundry pile.

TIME

New Orleans, LA. Present. Fat Tuesday.

Light drift up in the grimy light of a neighborhood hole-in-the-wall bar. SAMMIE is seated on a bar stool holding a giant, bejeweled shockingly red tomato purse. A full shot of whiskey on the bar.

SAMMIE: This year she was a giant tomato. A fat, luscious Creole tomato. And carried this purse. When we met she was dressed as a giant apple.

"I'm a crab apple." She said in her melodic southern accent. Trust me. There's nothing crabby about her.

PAUSE

Why should I do this?

I'm not like those other people gathering for this weird Mardi Gras ritual. They get together with their hoola-hoops, ribbons floating on breezes, costumes of satin, lace. Fur. Paint. Rubber. Spikes. Don't ask.

They start when the sun pushes over the twin bridges to warm the morning. And they're already drinking. Not that

that's a surprise to anyone in Marigny. Not to me. Not normally.

But today isn't normal.

And I don't have my hula-hoop. And I'm not in costume. It's only been forty-eight hours.

But some of them? They've been holding onto their ashes for months just waiting for today to pour them out into the blackness of the Mississippi. Watch them swirl with the current; breathe in the mixture of mud and frogs and humanity. And ashes.

Listen. Hear that? Storyville Stompers. You know their music.

(she sings) IT'S CARNIVAL TIME IN NEW ORLEANS.

PAUSE

I wasn't with her. I should have been there. But I wasn't. I went to the Orpheus parade early, lured by *their* music just as their God lured all living things with his. She could always lure me. With *her* music. With her eyes. With her laughter. With her…everything.

"Go on ahead. I'll be there in a few. I just need to sew on these last vines."

She never showed up.

Some people think its fun to shoot guns in the air during carnival. They never think about where the bullet will land.

And if I go with them? Pull myself away from this full shot of her favorite whiskey. Take this silly, sparkly tomato purse that is so her. Push out into the sun that I don't think I can feel on my skin anymore. And follow them to the river? I'll have to say goodbye.

Stupid fucking tradition. Pour the ashes of your dead in the Mississippi, let the ribbons sprinkle water from the river over you. Say good-bye. Say good-bye. Good-bye. As they float out to sea and you're left there, standing on the bank, wanting to jump in after them.

It's only been 48 hours. I don't have to be ready. Do I?

PAUSE

I'd rather take Creole tomato here and head over to Armstrong Park like we did every year since we met. I had just moved to New Orleans, to a ramshackle second floor walk-up on Esplanade...like lemonade. That's how she told me to say it so I didn't sound like a tourist. She lived on the first floor. And she lured me.

I thought Mardi Gras was just about the parties and drinking. And, sure, we enjoyed that part but she showed me the parts that make this place her home. Families staking out the same parade spots that their parents and grandparents held for decades. Gathering for the Krewe of Shut-Ins to bring parade joy to nursing home. Neighbors decorating their own trucks to march with each other. She helped sew beads on the truck banners. Like these bright red tomato ones. She loves...loved Carnival.

"Its part of the tradition." She told me that the first time she took me to the foot of Canal Street for St. Anne's ritual of honoring the dead. Of pouring those ashes.

Of pouring *these* ashes out of this bright red sparkly purse.

"The ghosts of those you've loved most are there."

She really believed that. That New Orleans is peopled with ghosts and St. Anne's has the most New Orleans way of saying good-bye. Ashes mixed with waters that form this city. Her people. My people. My...her.

PAUSE

The ghosts of those you've loved most are there.

PAUSE

Yes, if you're wondering. Its what she'd want.

And she lured me in.

And I'd do anything for her.

Even when I didn't want to.

Even when I wasn't ready.

Even if it means saying good-bye to the ashes and hello to her ghost.

Downs the whiskey in one shot. Kisses purse and exits with it.

Lights fade.

END OF PLAY

JOANIE & FREDDIE ON VALENTINE'S DAY

DEDICATED TO MY MOM & DAD, Joan and Fred George, and their eternal love. In 2015, they celebrated their 60th wedding anniversary.

When my mom was in 4th grade, my dad, being the rambunctious boy that he was, pushed the red-headed JOANIE into a snow bank. That act of youthful exuberance is what inspired this play. And although the rest of the story is a coming together of fact (my grandparents did divorce) and fiction (this Valentine's Day lives in my imagination), the love that is just beginning in this play is true to what my parents are and what they forever share with their family.

CAST OF CHARACTERS

JOANIE: 10 years old. She is usually boisterous and fun but is recently dealing with sorrow in her life. She is dressed in period middle-class winter-wear, carrying her schoolbooks in a leather strap over her shoulder. She also carries a box that holds a delicate Valentine's heart that she made in school.

FREDDIE: 12 years old. He is bold and all boy, athletic, silly, but also quick to anger. He is dressed in period winter-wear that reflects a poorer life than JOANIE. His clothes are covered in mud and snow from playing outside.

TIME

Valentine's Day. 1945.

SETTING

A snow-covered dirt path in a rural setting. Alongside the path is a giant snowbank that is slick with ice and snow.

The sound of children running and laughing is heard as lights come up in the blue glow of a cold February winter afternoon. JOANIE shuffles across stage, her schoolbooks slung over her shoulder as she carefully balances the box. FREDDIE runs on stage, throwing snowballs to off-stage friends.

FREDDIE: (yelling to off-stage) Ha! Right in the kisser! The Brooklyn Dodgers are gonna call me to replace Cy Buker and Clyde King both! (in a radio announcer voice) The starting Pitcher for the '45 season, Freddie George! (normal voice) Ha! See ya tomorrow!

FREDDIE dodges snowballs thrown at him, he spins, sees JOANIE, stops and smiles. He throws a snowball past her but she pays no attention. He throws another, she still ignores him. FREDDIE runs towards JOANIE, does a slide as if into 2nd base, knocks JOANIE into the snowbank as she comes out of one of her shoes.

JOANIE: Hey!

FREDDIE: (giggling) Sorry. Didn't see ya there.

JOANIE: Then you need glasses.

JOANIE tries to reach for her shoe but its too far away.

JOANIE: Gimme my shoe and help me up. I gotta get home for my dad...I just gotta get home now.

FREDDIE rises and chuckles.

FREDDIE: You look kinda funny all covered in snow. (teasing) Joanie is a snowman. Joanie is a snowman. Joanie is a - -

JOANIE balls up a quick snowball and throws it, hitting FREDDIE.

JOANIE: Cut that out and help me.

FREDDIE picks up her shoe and tosses it in the air.

FREDDIE: What if I don't?

JOANIE: Then my big brother Ray is gonna clobber you.

FREDDIE: Ray? I don't see no Ray around here. Guess you just gotta stay here and talk to me.

FREDDIE sits down in the snow next to her.

JOANIE: If I call him he'll come. (beat) Ray.

FREDDIE jumps up and back a bit, anticipating Ray's arrival.

PAUSE

JOANIE: Ray!

JOANIE and FREDDIE look off-stage.

JOANIE: RAAAAAAAAAAAAY!

FREDDIE kicks the snow.

FREDDIE: Like I said, don't see no Ray around here.

JOANIE: Then I'll call my brother Lou.

FREDDIE sits back down beside her.

FREDDIE: No you ain't even gonna do that. Everybody knows Lou is fighting the Nazis over in Germany.

JOANIE: Then I'll call Kenny. He's coming home from school same as me and he'll clobber you.

JOANIE: Kenny.

FREDDIE jumps up and back a bit, anticipating Kenny's arrival.

PAUSE

JOANIE: Kenny!

JOANIE and FREDDIE look off-stage.

JOANIE: KEEEEEEEEEENNY!

PAUSE

FREDDIE: Looks like you gotta stay here and talk to me.

JOANIE: Freddie George you're a fat-head! Get me out of this snowbank right now! If I miss my dad I'll clobber you myself!

FREDDIE: Geez-louise, don't flip your wig.

FREDDIE hands JOANIE her shoe. She puts it on and he reaches down and helps her up from the snowbank. As he does she sees the box is crushed. She gently opens it and takes out the broken Valentine's heart. JOANIE tries to put the pieces back together: she is visibly upset.

JOANIE: No. No. No. Look what you did.

FREDDIE: What the heck is it?

JOANIE: Nothing.

FREDDIE: If it's nothing then why ya balling?

JOANIE: Leave me alone. Fat-head.

JOANIE continues to try to put the Valentine back together.

FREDDIE: Lemme help.

JOANIE: Leave me alone or I'll call - -

FREDDIE: Ain't nobody else to call, Joanie, 'cept your dad and everybody knows - -

JOANIE: Knows what?

FREDDIE: What?

JOANIE: Knows what?

FREDDIE: Nothing.

JOANIE: What were you gonna say?

FREDDIE: Nothing. (beat as he softens) Gimme that. I can fix it.

JOANIE: I'm giving this to my dad.

FREDDIE: Sure you are.

JOANIE: I am. I don't care what you think. You don't know.

> FREDDIE holds out his hand. JOANIE hesitantly gives him the Valentine.

FREDDIE: Now if we just put this piece over here.

> FREDDIE takes an elastic band from his pocket and wraps it around the broken part of the heart. It fits together but flops over lopsided.

FREDDIE: That's better?

JOANIE: You ruined everything.

FREDDIE: I didn't mean to. I just wanted you to stay and talk with me, is all.

JOANIE: Why would I do that?

FREDDIE: Cuz.

JOANIE: Cuz why?

FREDDIE: Cuz you're kinda funny when you look like a snowman.

JOANIE: And you're doll-dizzy.

FREDDIE: Am not!

JOANIE: Are to!

FREDDIE: I don't like any girls. Not even you. Even. Not. So you can go home to your stupid brothers.

JOANIE: I'm going home to see my father.

FREDDIE shrugs his shoulders, kicks the snow.

JOANIE: Yes I am. You don't know. Fat-head!

FREDDIE: Stop calling me that.

JOANIE: Fat-head.

FREDDIE: Am not!

JOANIE: Fat-head. Fat-head!

FREDDIE: The whole neighborhood knows he left your ma last month!

PAUSE as JOANIE turns and starts walking away.

FREDDIE: (softens) Joanie? Oh. I really am a fat-head. I'm sorry. Please stay. Please. I just got mad. I didn't mean nothing.

JOANIE stops.

JOANIE: I made him this Valentine so maybe he'd come home today and he and my mom can make up and not get...not get a...

FREDDIE: You don't have to say nothing.

JOANIE: It was an ugly Valentine anyway.

FREDDIE: It's a cute Valentine.

JOANIE: Just paper and wire and red paint and dumb old glitter. The teacher made us all make one for our dads and I didn't want to look...stupid.

FREDDIE: You're not stupid. You're the smartest girl I know and you throw real good.

FREDDIE rubs the spot where JOANIE hit him with the earlier snowball.

Like a boy. If the Brooklyn Dodgers took girls, they'd be lucky to have you.

JOANIE: You're just saying that so I'll stop crying.

FREDDIE: Yeah. I mean…

PAUSE

I like your Valentine.

JOANIE: Really?

FREDDIE nods. JOANIE hands it out to him.

FREDDIE: What?

JOANIE: You can have it.

FREDDIE: Nah. It's for your dad.

JOANIE: I was hoping if I made this for him somehow he'd know. But he's not coming home.

JOANIE plops down in the snow.

JOANIE: They hate each other.

JOANIE puts the Valentine down in the snow.

JOANIE: I don't want them to get a…divorce. I don't know anybody who ever, ever had a divorce. Do you?

FREDDIE shakes his head 'no'.

JOANIE: And my brothers will go live with dad and I have to stay with mom and it's not fair. I'll never see them again.

FREDDIE plops down next to JOANIE.

FREDDIE: Sure ya will. And, hey, just think, now you got two families. Two Christmases. Two birthdays. I'll bet you even get double cakes and presents and stuff.

PAUSE as FREDDIE nudges JOANIE, reaches into his pocket and hands her a handkerchief. JOANIE loudly blows her nose into it and then hands it back to FREDDIE.

FREDDIE: Uh, you can keep it. (beat) I'm sorry about, ya know.

JOANIE: Thanks. (beat) I don't wanna go home.

PAUSE as FREDDIE grabs a bunch of snow and begins molding it.

FREDDIE: Wanna throw snowballs?

JOANIE shakes her head 'no'.

FREDDIE: Make snow angels?

JOANIE shakes her head 'no'.

FREDDIE: We could go ice skating.

JOANIE: I like to ice skate.

FREDDIE: Then let's go.

JOANIE: Is this just your way of making me stay and talk to you?

FREDDIE: Maybe. Would that be so bad?

JOANIE shakes her head 'no' and smiles. FREDDIE rises.

FREDDIE: Joanie?

JOANIE: Yeah?

FREDDIE hands her the snow he's been molding—it is in the shape of a heart.

FREDDIE: Happy Valentine's Day.

FREDDIE holds out his hand, helps JOANIE up, they walk off slowly, leaving the bent Valentine behind.

END OF PLAY

ABOUT THE AUTHOR

Playwright Charlene A. Donaghy's plays have been produced in New York City, Boston, St. Louis, Pittsburgh, Memphis, and in other cities around the United States, with recognition in Great Britain and Canada. Her full-length play, *The Quadroon and the Dove*, will premiere Off-Broadway produced by Madison Square Productions. Her play *Gift of an Orange*, inspired by Tennessee Williams short story *Gift of an Apple*, opened the season for Boston's New Urban Theatre Laboratory.

Ms. Donaghy's publications include *Best American Short Plays, Estrogenius, In the Eye, 25*10-Minute Plays for Teens, The Louisiana Literary Journal,* and the *Mad River Literary Journal.* Her recognitions and awards include international finalist for Great Britain's North American Actors Association Playreading Award, nominee for the National Partners in American Theatre Playwriting Award, a two-time John Cauble national semi-Finalist, a finalist for the Actors Theatre of Louisville Heideman Award, a finalist for Canada's Bottle Tree Productions, and other accolades.

Ms. Donaghy is Festival Director for the Warner International Playwrights Festival, Producing Director for the Provincetown Tennessee Williams Theater Festival, and Co-Producer of the Association for Theatre in Higher Education's New Play Development Workshop. She teaches in the University of Nebraska Omaha's MFA in Creative Writing and Department of Theatre. Ms. Donaghy is the Connecticut Regional Representative and member of The Dramatists Guild of America, The Playwrights Center, Association for Theatre in Higher Education, New York City's 9th Floor Playwrights' Collective, and she is a founding member of Boston's Proscenium Playwrights. Ms. Donaghy is a breast cancer survivor and holds true to Tennessee Williams' words from *Camino Real* "Make Voyages! Attempt them! There's nothing else." www.charleneadonaghy.com